# HOW TO WRITE

## A NEW KILLER ACT ESSAY

### TOM CLEMENTS

HIT 'EM UP PUBLISHING
CALIFORNIA 2015

HIT 'EM UP Publishing
tctutoring
346 Rheem Blvd. , Suite 110-B
Moraga, CA 94556


First Edition: September, 2015

Cover design by Namita Kapoor

Special thanks to Sachi, Sumi, Suki, Niki and, of course, Michi

Printed in the United States of America
ISBN: 0578169312

≡
_____

Visit my website at: www.tctutoring.net

Visit my youtube channel for new-ACT-essay videos:
www.youtube.com/tctutoring

## Killer SAT Essay Book

To dominate the SAT Essay check out my other book:

How to Write a Killer SAT Essay

## Preface

We shall not cease from exploration
And the end of all our exploring
Will be to arrive where we started
And know the place for the first time

T. S. Eliot

# Table of Contents ☰

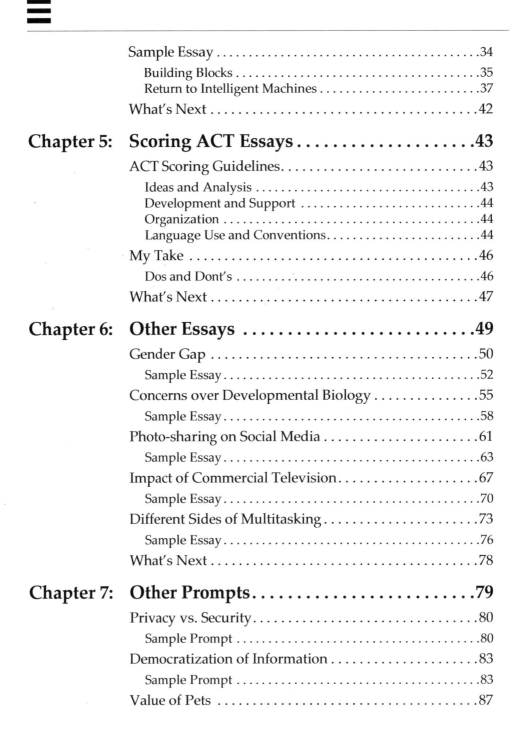

# 1—The Prompt

As a prospective test taker for the NEW ACT essay — or the parent of a test taker, or a professional ACT tutor — the first question you should ask yourself when debating the purchase of a manual is this: Why should I buy this book? How does it differ from other ACT books on the market? Well, OK, that's two questions but they're equally valid. Here's why:

- Most ACT manuals try to cover *everything* on the test, paying only cursory attention to the essay. This book deals *only* with the NEW essay and provides a clear and comprehensive methodology that any student can use to quickly compose a top-scoring essay.

- As part of this methodology, visual reference points in the form of T-charts are provided to help you parse the prompt — the ACT topic — quickly and confidently into pro and con arguments, around which you can organize your essay.

- Real essays from real students are provided, offering you dramatic insight into how the simple tips described in this book have been put into actual practice in top-scoring essays.

In a minute, we'll delve into parsing the prompt and describing the methodology behind top-scoring essays. But first, just so you know what you're getting into, a few words on the general structure of the ACT are in order.

## ACT Structure

The ACT is comprised of five parts: Writing, Math, Reading, the dreaded Science section and the new forty-minute essay. Although the NEW ACT essay is presented as an *optional* part of the test, many schools refuse to recognize ACT scores unless accompanied by the essay. If you are absolutely certain that the only colleges and universities on your academic dance card are those that don't require the essay, then you don't need this book. For the rest of you, the essay is mandatory. Better safe than sorry.

Unlike the SAT, which tends to be a chess game, the ACT is a more like a track meet. Students are required to move at top speed through each section. No time for second-guessing or overly slow, cumbersome analysis. Top scores work at top speeds!

- Writing

    Grammar — Four short narratives presented, 75 questions posed and a total of 45 minutes provided.

- Math

    Algebra, geometry, trigonometry — 60 mostly straightforward, classroom-based math questions with a total of 60 minutes provided. One question per minute. Not too bad if you've paid attention in school.

- Reading

    Texts — Four types of passages presented: prose, social science, humanities and natural science, each containing 10 questions for a total of 40 questions posed in a total of 35 minutes. Ouch!

- Science

    Data — Seven passages drawn from various science areas are presented. Not so much science as data interpretation; but a working knowledge of chemistry, physics and biology certainly helps. The emphasis is placed on numeric correlation of information contained in charts, graphs and tables. 40 questions posed and a total of 35 minutes provided. Brutal!

- "Optional" NEW Essay

    Composition — The NEW ACT essay presents students with a topic that can be approached from multiple points of view. The prompt sets the stage by delineating contrasting positions. Three "perspectives" — which is to say three different points of view — on the topic are also provided.

    Students must isolate the contrasts in the prompt and take either pro or con positions on the perspectives provided.

    This is a new type of essay, which many students will find daunting. However, the methodology set forth in this book will help you overcome your initial anxiety and learn to produce a top-scoring essay.

# The Prompt

Every ACT Essay begins with a prompt that discusses some question that can be broken down into opposing points of view. The first order of business, then, is to map out the basic issues presented in the prompt and develop pro and con arguments into a T-chart.

Three different perspectives on the prompt are provided by the ACT, and students must determine whether they agree or disagree with each perspective. To obtain a top score on the essay, it's important to think of concrete examples that can be used to support your case. Your essay will be graded not only on your writing and analytical skills but also on your ability to provide specific examples that buttress your arguments.

Both the prompt and the three perspectives present contrasting points of view. For this reason students must be able to handle BOTH sides of an issue, showing objectivity in their analysis and logic in support of their positions. The ability to handle opposing points of view is the mark of an unbiased and outstanding ACT essay.

Here's a sample ACT prompt with "dueling" points of view:

Intelligent Machines

> Many of the goods and services we depend on daily are now supplied by intelligent, automated machines rather than human beings. Robots build cars and other goods on assembly lines, where once there were human workers. Many of our phone conversations are now conducted not with people but with sophisticated technologies. We can now buy goods at a variety of stores without the help of a human cashier. Automation is generally seen as a sign of progress, but what is lost when we replace humans with machines? Given the accelerating variety and prevalence of intelligent machines, it is worth examining the implications and meaning of their presence in our lives.
>
> *Read and carefully consider these perspectives. Each suggests a particular way of thinking about the increasing presence of intelligent machines.*

Right away you can see lines being drawn between contrasting points of view:

- Intelligent machines are a sign of progress and efficiency
- But what is lost when we replace humans with machines?

Students must navigate between these conflicting points of view in their essays by devising supporting arguments for each.

Moreover, three different perspectives on the prompt are provided. Students must evaluate and determine pro and con positions for each of these perspectives, using concrete examples wherever possible.

At first, this may seem like a daunting proposition. But don't worry, using the T-chart technique described in the following chapters, you'll be able to parse the prompt quickly into *pros* and *cons*. You can also construct a Perspectives-chart to analyze the different perspectives, and get off to a jump-start on your essay.

## White Space

Once you've been presented with the prompt, you're provided with four pages of white space to generate your essay.

**Four pages of white space**

Although four pages are provided, it's not necessary to fill them all. However, to obtain a top score from the ACT Readers, you must fill in *at least two* of the pages completely and, *preferably, some portion of the third*. The point, really, is to fill up enough white space to equal **at least 450 words**. Filling all four pages is possible only if you have a robotic arm and the ability to trance-channel Jack Kerouac.

Top-scoring essays are invariably judged as much by length as by persuasive prose, logical analysis and supporting detail.

## ACT Readers — Who are These People?

The ACT recruits high school and college teachers (typically, English teachers) to grade your essay, giving it a score from "1" to "6". Since two Readers are assigned to each essay, the top composite score is "12".

Because the essay is "optional", your score is included as a separate entry with your ACT results. The essay, consequently, has no bearing on the Writing portion of your ACT.

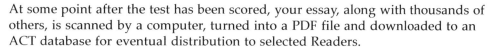

At some point after the test has been scored, your essay, along with thousands of others, is scanned by a computer, turned into a PDF file and downloaded to an ACT database for eventual distribution to selected Readers.

Each Reader receives a batch of essays and begins the scoring process. But don't expect the Readers to grade your essay as a high school teacher might. No surplus of red ink, no meticulous attention to detail.

Readers get paid by the hour and the more essays they grade, the more chance they have of being invited back to participate in future essay-grading marathons. Therefore, the incentive for the Reader is to move through each essay as swiftly as possible, spending only a few minutes per essay.

That's right. Your Reader takes a leisurely stroll down essay lane, grading your prose in a LOT less time than it took you to write it.

On the surface, this may seem twisted and unfair, but you can make it work to your advantage. Knowing ACT Readers prefer to work fast, you can structure your essay to help them do just that.

Two things are essential in this regard. You must:

- Make a good first impression with your opening paragraph.
- Use clear transitions throughout your essay so that the Reader can follow, Oz-like, your yellow-brick writing road.

Chapter 3 presents a sample prompt with perspectives and a complete essay that incorporates and expands on the introductory points made in this chapter.

## What's Next

In the next chapter, we'll take a look at the three Perspectives that accompany the prompt. Your job is to summarize the points of view presented, agree or disagree with the presentation and support your analysis with concrete detail.

We'll also take a look at the Rules of Engagement: the seven rules all writers need to compose high quality prose.

# 2—Perspectives

As Marcus Aurelius pointed out two millennia ago, "Everything we hear is an opinion, not a fact. Everything we see is a perspective, not the truth."

Both soldier and philosopher, Marcus Aurelius was way ahead of his time when it comes to planning for the ACT Essay since, strictly speaking, the essay is really just a **matter of perspective** — three of them to be exact, which is what the ACT provides you for every prompt. Three different takes from three different points of view. Students have to take sides and argue pro or con on each of the three positions.

## Three Perspectives

Here are the three perspectives provided for the sample prompt — *intelligent machines* — that we saw in Chapter 1.

| Perspective One | Perspective Two | Perspective Three |
|---|---|---|
| What we lose with the replacement of people by machines is some part of our own humanity. Even our mundane daily encounters no longer require from us basic courtesy, respect, and tolerance for other people. | Machines are good at low-skill, repetitive jobs, and at high-speed, extremely precise jobs. In both cases they work better than humans. This efficiency leads to a more prosperous and progressive world for everyone. | Intelligent machines challenge our long-standing ideas about what humans are or can be. This is good because it pushes both humans and machines toward new, unimagined possibilities. |

In the previous incarnation of the ACT essay — that is, before September, 2015 — it was enough just to write **your own** opinions and support them with concrete examples.

For the NEW ACT essay, however, you have to evaluate the opinions/perspectives of others and then support or deride those opinions with concrete examples of your own.

Harrison Ford in "The Raiders of the Lost Ark" famously quipped: "I'm making this up as I go along." That's OK for Harrison but not for students aspiring to a top score on their ACT essay. This is a different kind of ball game — imagination alone is not enough.

On the NEW ACT essay you are presented with the opinions of *others* — your job is to analyze and critique *those* perspectives. Now, this doesn't mean that you can't bring imagination to bear on the analysis. It just means that the analysis comes first and your (perhaps imaginative) response comes second.

In some sense this makes the job easier: you don't have to make stuff up, you just have to comment intelligently on what someone else has already made up for you. Let's take, for example, the first perspective provided on the previous page:

**Perspective One**

What we lose with the replacement of people by machines is some part of our own humanity. Even our mundane daily encounters no longer require from us basic courtesy, respect, and tolerance for other people.

This perspective can be easily summarized in a few words like this: *humanity is lost when machines replace people.*

After summarizing the perspective, your job is to agree or disagree with the point of view. Usually, it's easier to agree than disagree so let's assume you go along with the idea. Now comes the hard part: you have to support your viewpoint by coming up with CONCRETE EXAMPLES that demonstrate the logic of your position. You need to marshall all available arguments in favor of the perspective.

You might, for example, talk about how Internet applications like Twitter or Snapchat are short-lived, shallow forms of communication that disrupt and short-change the development of deep human relations. Or you might want to cite specific examples from retail stores where busy clerks hardly look up from their computers to interact with customers.

Whatever the case, be sure to keep your prose grounded in reality by using real-world CONCRETE EXAMPLES. Don't write wishy-washy abstract sentences to support your position. Get down and dirty with specific examples comprised of as much detail as possible. Remember, good writing — and top-scoring ACT essays — are full of details, details, details. Your essay will be graded not only on your writing and analytical skills but also on your ability to provide specific examples that buttress your arguments.

Once you've parsed the prompt and determined pro and con positions on the three perspectives, then it's just a matter of implementing some simple *Rules of Engagement* to ensure a top-scoring essay. These rules are presented in this chapter as a general writing methodology that has proven successful for hundreds of my former students.

**Note:** For a more detailed look at the specific criteria the ACT uses to score essays, see Chapter 5, "Scoring ACT Essays."

## Rules of Engagement — Seven Criteria

There are seven commonly-agreed upon criteria for judging good writing. These include:

- Introduction

   All ACT prompts are built as contrasting points of view. Your introduction should both describe the contrast and establish context for the essay. Quotes and anecdotes are a common way to embellish introductory paragraphs since they set the scene for the central arguments of the essay.

- Structure

   Your essay should follow a classic five to seven paragraph format; that is, an introductory paragraph that sets the scene, three to five body paragraphs taking either pro or con positions on the perspectives provided, and a conclusion. Because the ACT essay demands comparison and contrast, you can use multiple body paragraphs to shift between conflicting points of view.

- Transitions

   Your essay must have smooth transitions both *between* paragraphs and *within* paragraphs. Intelligent transitions, the mark of a good writer in general, are particularly important on the ACT essay, where pro and con positions on both the prompt and the perspectives must be clearly delineated.

   A detailed look at transitions is provided at the end of this chapter.

- Subordination

   Good prose style is characterized by heavy use of subordination. Subordination lends variety to your writing style by replacing short, choppy, subject-verb-object sentences with longer, more elegant sentences that incorporate dependent clauses.

   Subordination, in a nutshell, is a way to ensure sentence variety in your writing style. The more subordination, the more sophisticated the prose.

A detailed look at subordination is provided at the end of this chapter.

- Flash Vocabulary

  An extensive vocabulary is the mark of a good writer. Remember that part of your job on the ACT essay is to impress the reader with your use of interesting and sophisticated vocab sprinkled throughout your essay.

- Details, Details, Details

  The devil, as they always say, is in the details. Nowhere is this more important than in ACT writing. Two reasons: first of all, you have to fill up as much white space as possible to obtain a top score; second, the more detail you provide in your essay, the more compelling the narrative.

  To avoid wishy-washy abstract writing — and a low scoring essay — put some teeth into your prose by presenting concrete descriptions with finely focused analysis. Top scoring ACT essays typically run close to 450 words. Size matters!

- Narrative Cohesion and Logical Flow

  These two go hand-in-hand. Good transitions assure logical flow and logical flow assures narrative cohesion.

  The hallmark of a top-scoring essay is not just a bunch of facts strung together in linear formation. Top scoring ACT essays exhibit a cohesive narrative flow where diverse viewpoints meld together harmoniously and a strong common thread runs throughout.

In ensuing chapters, I'll elaborate on how to incorporate these clear and simple writing principles into your essay to ensure a top score from the readers. For now, I want to highlight in a little more detail two of the techniques mentioned above.

## Transitions

Because the ACT provides prompts with multiple points of view, good writers need to make copious use of transitions, which allow ACT Readers to follow the narrative flow of the composition.

You see this all the time in good writing. Transition words like "consequently" and "therefore" help the reader understand the logical sequencing of the composition. Transition words like "however" and "on the other hand" are employed to emphasize a change in direction in the argument.

When grading essays, ACT readers, much like all standardized test graders, prefer a guided tour through your essay; they hate unnecessary digressions and unwarranted zig-zags. They want to get through your prose as quickly as possible. You're going to spend 40 minutes pouring out your opinions — and heart and soul — in your essay; however, the readers may only take a few minutes scoring your essay.

Transition words, as we'll see later, can be used both *within* paragraphs and *between* paragraphs; they're like signposts on a highway, clearly delineating for the Reader the logical twists and turns in the development of your essay. Moreover, transitions are the mark of a mind that knows how to handle both sides of an argument, an attribute essential to top-scoring ACT essays.

Following is a list of common transitions, divided into those that propel the narrative forward (pro) and those that signify a counterpoint (con) or reverse direction to the argument. Keep this list in mind. In fact, you might want to circle it here and/or dog ear this page. As we'll see in the next chapter, transitions are a great complement to perspectives on the prompt.

**List of Transitions**

| Pro | Con |
| --- | --- |
| consequently | however |
| therefore | on the other hand |
| along the same lines | in contrast to |
| in fact | ironically |
| furthermore | although |
| in addition | yet |
| moreover | despite |
| clearly | unfortunately |
| to ensure this | to take issue with that |
| on top of that | but |

# Subordination

Since the ACT essay is a writing test, sentence variety (subordination) is essential to a top score. Bad writers compose sentences with little narrative flow, simple subject-verb-object concoctions that don't carry much punch.

Good writers use subordination to lend variety to their writing style by replacing short, choppy, subject-verb-object sentences with longer, more elegant sentences that incorporate dependent and independent clauses.

Take the following examples of two boring subject-verb-object sentences stuck together with a period.

> Mahatma Ghandi decided on a hunger strike to fight British Colonialism. He inspired the India Independence movement.

Functional but boring. There are three different ways to rearrange and subordinate these choppy sentences to make them more interesting. For example:

- After deciding on a hunger strike to fight British Colonialism, Mahatma Ghandi inspired the India Independence movement.

  Notice the long lead-in *After deciding on a hunger strike to fight British Colonialism,* which now precedes the subject of the sentence, Mahatma Ghandi. This is a much better use of sentence variety.

- Mahatma Ghandi, an inspiration to the India Independence movement, decided on a hunger strike to fight British Colonialism.

  In this example, the inserted phrase *an inspiration to the India Independence movement* is now sandwiched, to much greater effect, between the main subject and verb of the sentence.

- Mahatma Ghandi decided on a hunger strike to fight British Colonialism, inspiring the India Independence movement.

  In this example, the tag-along to the main clause *inspiring the India Independence movement* is now placed at the end of the sentence, creating smoother sentence flow.

The key point to remember is that good writing is all about narrative flow. Without subordination, sentences sit on the page like patients tranquilized upon a table. Healthy sentences, like healthy people, need to breathe, to move, to dance, to flow. Subordination makes it so.

## What's Next

In the next chapter, we'll put these ideas into play with an essay based on the sample prompt and perspectives discussed in the first two chapters. We'll see how to use a T-chart to parse the prompt into pro and con positions, helping us to jump-start the essay. Then we'll construct a Perspectives-chart to analyze the three different points of view that accompany the prompt. Finally, we'll compose a complete sample essay. Stay tuned.

# 3—Sample Essay

In this chapter, we'll construct an ACT essay based on the sample prompt and perspectives discussed in the previous two chapters.

Before any writing begins, students should analyze the prompt and consider the perspectives provided. As noted earlier, the prompt will always center on a contrast. Isolate the contrast and you're half way to success. The ACT actually helps you get started on the rest of your essay by suggesting various points of view.

Remember: the ACT is all about diverse perspectives. You can either agree or disagree with the perspectives but you must include an analysis of each in the body of your essay. Be sure to support your analysis with concrete details. Recall that high scoring ACT essays are grounded in details, details, details.

Previously, we examined the prompt in sections. Here it's presented with all sections intact. We'll parse the prompt, marshall sub-arguments, add perspectives and construct a sample essay based on our analysis.

## Intelligent Machines

Many of the goods and services we depend on daily are now supplied by intelligent, automated machines rather than human beings. Robots build cars and other goods on assembly lines, where once there were human workers. Many of our phone conversations are now conducted not with people but with sophisticated technologies. We can now buy goods at a variety of stores without the help of a human cashier. Automation is generally seen as a sign of progress, but what is lost when we replace humans with machines? Given the accelerating variety and prevalence of intelligent machines, it is worth examining the implications and meaning of their presence in our lives.

*Read and carefully consider these perspectives. Each suggests a particular way of thinking about the increasing presence of intelligent machines.*

| Perspective One | Perspective Two | Perspective Three |
|---|---|---|
| What we lose with the replacement of people by machines is some part of our own humanity. Even our mundane daily encounters no longer require from us basic courtesy, respect, and tolerance for other people. | Machines are good at low-skill, repetitive jobs, and at high-speed, extremely precise jobs. In both cases they work better than humans. This efficiency leads to a more prosperous and progressive world for everyone. | Intelligent machines challenge our long-standing ideas about what humans are or can be. This is good because it pushes both humans and machines toward new, unimagined possibilities. |

### Essay Task

Write a unified, coherent essay in which you evaluate multiple perspectives on the increasing presence of intelligent machines. In your essay, be sure to:

- analyze and evaluate the perspectives given

- state and develop your own perspective on the issue

- explain the relationship between your perspective and those given

Your perspective may be in full agreement with any of the others, in partial agreement, or wholly different. Whatever the case, support your ideas with logical reasoning and detailed, persuasive examples.

## Planning Your Essay

The ACT organization gives you some general advice about how you should approach your essay. You should, for example, examine the introduction and pay close attention to the strengths and weaknesses of the three perspectives given. In addition, you should have some personal perspective on the issues presented and be able to support and develop that perspective in the body of your essay.

The first order of business, then, is to map out the basic issues presented in the prompt and develop pro and con arguments in a T-chart.

## Isolate the Contrast

The prompt gives you a running start on your essay by introducing a theme with broad brush-strokes, making it easy to isolate contrasting points of view. Think back on the first paragraph of the prompt for *Intelligent Machines* and hone in on this sentence:

> Automation is generally seen as a sign of progress, but what is lost when we replace humans with machines?

Every ACT essay prompt — indeed, most literature — revolves around contrast. Isolate the contrast and you're ready to parse the prompt.

In this case, and in most cases, it's fairly easy to split the general introduction into pro and con arguments with a simple T-chart. For example:

| Pro | Con |
| --- | --- |
| Intelligent machines are a sign of progress and efficiency. | What is lost when we replace humans with machines? |

You can use these contrasting points of view to conceptualize and organize the themes of your essay. You can also bank off of these for sub-arguments that will lend your introductory paragraph context and punch. For example:

| Sub-arguments | |
| --- | --- |
| Robots build cars fast and efficiently on assembly lines | Use "I, Robot" movie for perils of automation |
| ATMS make it quick and easy to do banking transactions | Phone and Internet conversations now done with machines |

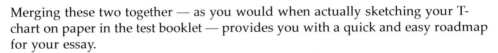

Merging these two together — as you would when actually sketching your T-chart on paper in the test booklet — provides you with a quick and easy roadmap for your essay.

| Pro | Con |
|---|---|
| Intelligent machines are a sign of progress and efficiency. | What is lost when we replace humans with machines? |
| **Sub-arguments** | **Sub-arguments** |
| Robots build cars fast and efficiently on assembly lines | Use "I, Robot" movie for perils of automation |
| ATM machines make it quick and easy to do banking transactions | Phone and Internet conversations now done with machines |

Notice that while some of the sub-arguments are drawn directly from the prompt, others are either extrapolations of the theme (ATM machines) or imaginative images ("I, Robot") that can be used to give depth and insight to your essay.

It's important to both expound on the information provided and to use your creative energies to enhance and enlarge upon it.

Finally, you'll want to consider the three perspectives provided by the ACT and determine whether you agree or disagree with each perspective. Hint: it's usually easier, given the thirty-minute time constraint of the essay, to agree; adventurous souls, however, can agree to disagree.

Once you determine your positions in regard to each perspective, it's important to think of concrete examples you can use to support your case. Your essay will be graded not only on your writing and analytical skills but also on your ability to provide specific examples that buttress your arguments. Bad writers write in bland generalities and fail to bring their abstract ideas down to earth. Good writers know how to stick it!

To start your analysis, first tease out the main point of each perspective, then attach concrete examples to support whatever position you plan to take. This gives you a Perspectives-chart to go along with your T-chart. For example:

| Perspectives Chart |
|---|
| **Perspective One**<br>Lose our humanity when machines replace people<br><br>CONCRETE EXAMPLES: Internet applications replace human contact and face-to-face interaction — retail clerks rude and disinterested<br><br>**Perspective Two**<br>Machines are good at high speed tasks and efficiency leads to prosperity<br><br>CONCRETE EXAMPLES: Stock market and banking — Nasa and space exploration<br><br>**Perspective Three**<br>Machines and humans work together toward unimagined possibilities<br><br>CONCRETE EXAMPLES: Cash dispensing machines, Netfix, Self-driving cars — use pro and con positions to create inspirational conclusion |

Of course, there are many other approaches we could use to clarify and ground our analysis, but these are fairly straightforward examples that address the prompt in an intelligent and useful manner.

**Note:** For an alternative take on this process, see Chapter 4, where one of my students handles this sample prompt with entirely different examples.

All this parsing of the prompt, evaluation of perspectives and construction of T-charts should take you no more than 5 to 10 minutes, after which you'll have a rough outline/roadmap for your essay.

Moreover, feel free to vary your positions on these perspectives during the actual writing when and if insight and imagination produce other ideas. But rest assured you have a strong and solid starting point that you can leverage and bank off of when new ideas emerge.

≡

Having organized the key points of your essay, you're now armed and dangerous and ready to write. You've mapped out the general arguments. You've analyzed the specific perspectives given. You've listed concrete examples to support (or not) the perspectives provided. Now let's see how to put all these component pieces into play.

## Sample Essay

*Intelligent Machines*

A common theme of science fiction has been the conflict between man and machine. In the recent film, "I, Robot", the protagonist, Will Smith, ends up doing battle against intelligent robots who have dropped their facade of "obedient compliance" and rebelled against their human masters. Today, science fiction is becoming science fact, although not to the extreme presented in the movie. Instead, we have docile machines programmed for efficiencies. Rather than running amok, today's machines are either fixed in place like ATM machines or operating as software interfaces to telephones or the Internet.

But are these machines, programmed for fast, smart and efficient operations causing us to lose human perspective on events? From a personal point of view, I find myself more attached to my iPhone than to the people around me. I'd rather text than talk. Moreover, Internet apps like SnapChat and Instagram don't really let people communicate deeply. These machine driven apps are short-lived. The so-called conversation is gone before it's had a chance to develop.

Things were simpler for us back when the human touch was more commonplace. Even clerks in retail stores seem to have been negatively impacted by the rise of machine technology. Some take our money and type our information into their consoles without even looking up, much less engaging us in conversation. Our mundane daily encounters with retail clerks at department stores like Sears or Walmart no longer require basic courtesy and respect. And who hasn't suffered the extreme frustration of being trapped in a phone maze, where a fake computer voice directs you through an endless chain of options until you finally close in on your destination, only to be greeted with a busy signal!

On the other hand, intelligent machines have streamlined business operations, automating various stock market transactions on Wall Street, making the ticker tape a relic of the past. From an efficiency perspective, machines are good at high-speed, extremely precise jobs. The space program, in particular, has benefitted from the rise of intelligent machines. We can now outfit space stations and send probes to Jupiter and Mars. Nasa recently, with pinpoint accuracy, landed a remote spacecraft on a comet streaming through the universe at 84,000 miles per hour.

The jury, however, is still out in terms of the ultimate effect, positive or negative, intelligent machines will have on humans. For every bank teller displaced by an ATM, there's a potential opening in the bank's expanding data center. For every video store clerk displaced by Netflix, however, the outlook is not so optimistic. Unhappily, there's

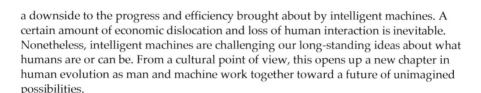

a downside to the progress and efficiency brought about by intelligent machines. A certain amount of economic dislocation and loss of human interaction is inevitable. Nonetheless, intelligent machines are challenging our long-standing ideas about what humans are or can be. From a cultural point of view, this opens up a new chapter in human evolution as man and machine work together toward a future of unimagined possibilities.

So there you have it. A complete ACT essay from start to finish. Now, to pull back the curtain and see what's really going on inside, the next section breaks this essay down into the building blocks that went into its construction.

## Building Blocks

As we've seen, every ACT essay is really just a series of building blocks stacked one on top of the other. One of the tricks to writing an essay in forty minutes or less is knowing how to assemble these blocks quickly into a cohesive whole.

In this section, we walk through the sample essay from start to finish, highlighting the function of each of the major building blocks and showing, with snippets from the essay, how that function is put into play.

### Introductory Paragraph

The introduction of the essay sets the scene by *isolating the contrast* in the first sentence — the conflict between man and machine. A popular science fiction movie is used to give a graphic illustration of the problems inherent in man/machine interaction. Then, as the narrative shifts from science fiction to science fact, the emphasis is placed on some of the positive contributions machines make to human society.

It's important to note that good writers always embellish their introductory paragraphs with either quotes, anecdotes or both. Anecdotes enliven the intro by placing themes in vivid contexts, in this case that of a science fiction movie.

By bringing in external information to enliven and enhance their themes, good writers produce provocative essays.

A quote, if you can think of one, will often work just as well as an anecdote to establish context. For example, the essay intro could have just as easily employed a quote from Erich Fromm to set the scene:

> The danger of the past was that men became slaves. The danger of the future is that man may become robots.

As you can see, this would have been an equally valid way to introduce the conflict between man and machine.

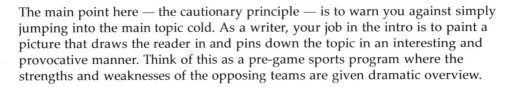

The main point here — the cautionary principle — is to warn you against simply jumping into the main topic cold. As a writer, your job in the intro is to paint a picture that draws the reader in and pins down the topic in an interesting and provocative manner. Think of this as a pre-game sports program where the strengths and weaknesses of the opposing teams are given dramatic overview.

### First Body Paragraph

The first body paragraph of the sample essay (after the introduction) supports Perspective One by fleshing out the points made in the outline. Internet applications, for example, are made specific with references to SnapChat and Instagram.

The theme of the perspective — loss of humanity — is emphasized by the shallow, short-lived quality of the communication that transpires on Internet devices.

From a stylistic point of view, notice the rhetorical device that opens the paragraph:

> But are these machines, programmed for fast, smart and efficient operations causing us to lose human perspective on events?

Rhetorical questions are a sophisticated way for writers to get their points across by inviting the reader to engage directly in the conversation.

Finally, notice the use of personal perspective in the second sentence of this paragraph.

> From a personal point of view, I find myself more attached to my iPhone than to the people around me.

Good writers have a detailed list of perspectives, or points of view, in their Bag of Tricks. To name just a few:

- From a financial perspective . . .
- From a personal perspective . . .
- From an academic perspective . . .
- From a psychological perspective . . .
- From a cultural perspective . . .

These are valuable both as transitions between paragraphs and as pointers within paragraphs that help readers better follow the arguments presented.

As stylistic devices, they clarify the direction taken by the narrative. Moreover, sometimes these linguistic perspectives merge with the perspectives presented in the ACT prompt, in which case writers can kill two birds with one stone. In the paragraph above, for example, the personal perspective both enhances the narrative and supports the writer's contention that machines reduce face-to-face contact with a resulting loss of humanity.

## Second Body Paragraph

The second body paragraph continues this line of thought and adds additional concrete examples regarding the negative effects of technology impacting clerks in retail stores.

> Our mundane daily encounters with retail clerks at department stores like Sears or Walmart no longer require basic courtesy and respect.

Again, from a stylistic perspective, notice how the next sentence in this paragraph gives graphic testimony to the underlying theme by drawing the reader into a universally frustrating experience, that of the phone maze:

> And who hasn't suffered the extreme frustration of being trapped in a phone maze, where a fake computer voice directs you through an endless chain of options until you finally close in on your destination, only to be greeted with a busy signal!

## Third Body Paragraph

The third body paragraph of this sample essay presents a counter-argument, which the author initiates like this:

> On the other hand, intelligent machines have streamlined business operations, automating various stock market transactions on Wall Street, making the ticker tape a relic of the past.

This introduces the *concession paragraph*, which is essential for top-scoring essays since it shows the ACT readers that you are conversant with both sides of an issue and can present arguments from multiple points of view. The concession paragraph is actually pretty easy to set up for two reasons:

1. The prompt itself presents two contrasting points — sooner or later you have to address these in your essay

2. Two of the three perspectives given along with the prompt present opposing points of view

In other words, composing a concession paragraph is pretty much a no-brainer. I just bring it up for students who are not in the habit of addressing more than one point of view.

That having been said, now notice how the writer uses a transition — *on the other hand* — to differentiate this paragraph from the preceding ones. Transitions like this, as we saw in Chapter 2, are important devices in guiding the reader through the sometimes turbulent waters of a pro and con essay.

Equally important as a stylistic device is the continued use of perspectives as narrative transitions, which both encapsulate point of view and allow readers to easily follow the thrust of the argument:

> From an efficiency perspective, machines are good at high-speed extremely precise jobs.

The author sums up the concession paragraph with a sentence loaded with concrete detail:

> We can now outfit space stations and send probes to Jupiter and Mars. Nasa recently, with pinpoint accuracy, landed a remote spacecraft on a comet streaming through the universe at 84,000 miles per hour.

## Conclusion

The concluding paragraph emphasizes the ambiguity inherent in the prompt:

> The jury, however, is still out in terms of the ultimate effect, positive or negative, intelligent machines will have on humans.

It then goes on to summarize the arguments for and against intelligent machines. You conclusion will always be a recap of the points made earlier in the essay.

Moreover, in this case, the conclusion actually addresses the third perspective, where machines, working in tandem with humans, may push humans to greater, unimagined possibilities. Always nice to end with a flourish:

> From a cultural point of view, this opens up a new chapter in human evolution as man and machine work together toward a future of unimagined possibilities.

*Opinions*

On a side note, be careful about injecting *unfounded* opinions in your essay. Your opinions are valid AS LONG AS you support them with compelling evidence.

To return to the quote from Marcus Aurelius in the beginning of this book:

> Everything we see is a perspective, not the truth.

Your opinions become vital to the narrative truth of the essay *if and only* if they're infused with sufficient supporting details and external facts to make them real. Vague opinions and generalities will NOT produce a top-scoring essay.

## Chapter Overview

Here's a recap on the main points of this chapter:

1. Construct a T-chart to isolate the contrast, parsing the prompt into pro and con positions

2. Generate sub-arguments for the T-chart based on the pro and con positions in the prompt

3. Construct a second chart to analyze and agree/disagree with the perspectives given

4. Attach CONCRETE EXAMPLES to the Perspectives-chart to support both your position and the perspectives that you are arguing for or against

5. Make sure to include a concession paragraph to balance your narrative

6. Employ transitions between and within paragraphs to help organize the essay and produce a smooth and logical narrative flow

7. Generate a conclusion which summarizes the points presented and makes a compelling case for your main argument or arguments.

## What's Next

In the next chapter we'll take a look at a second prompt with a similar format to show how prompts and essays are all variations on a common ACT theme.

# 4—Variations on a Theme

True or false? All ACT prompts are different. Well, yes and no. On the one hand, they all *appear* different, with different topics and different perspectives. But if you look closely at several ACT prompts, you'll see they're very similar under the surface. They all present pro and con views on some hot topic and they all demand analysis of different, often conflicting, points of view.

In this chapter we'll take a look at a second prompt similar in format to "Intelligent Machines." The same methodology will apply. In the beginning stages of any new endeavor, it helps to have repetition of the main ideas and techniques to build confidence and take ownership. Here we go.

## Sample Prompt

### Genetically Modified Foods

Many of the agricultural products and foods we consume daily are now produced by large farms whose genetic material has been altered through modern biotechnology engineering techniques. Researchers create combinations of plant, animal, bacteria, and viral genes for food products that would not exist naturally, where once there were simple, farm-made products. We can now manipulate foods to increase nutrient components and resistance to pests. This technology is generally seen as a sign of progress, but what is lost when we replace natural foods with modified organisms? Given the accelerating variety and prevalence of genetically modified organisms (GMOs), it is worth examining the implication and meaning of their presence in our lives.

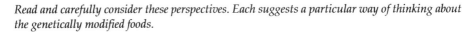

*Read and carefully consider these perspectives. Each suggests a particular way of thinking about the genetically modified foods.*

| Perspective One | Perspective Two | Perspective Three |
|---|---|---|
| We lose the ability to choose what we eat when genetically modified crops insinuate themselves into natural farming practices. This results in a loss of understanding about what consumers are actually buying when GMO goods populate grocery shelves. | Genetically modified organisms are good at boosting yields on crops. They also increase plant resistance to cold and drought, while providing nutrients that would not otherwise exist within the food. This efficiency leads to a more prosperous and progressive world. | Genetically modified organisms challenge our long-standing ideas about what food can provide nutritionally and the impact of food production on the environment. This pushes both researchers and consumers toward new unimagined possibilities. |

## Planning Your Essay

As before — and, hereafter, *as usual* — the first order of business is to map out the basic issues presented in the prompt and develop pro and con arguments in a T-chart.

## Isolate the Contrast

ACT prompts give you a running start on your essay by introducing a theme with contrasting points of view. Think back on the first paragraph of this sample prompt and hone in on this sentence:

> This technology is generally seen as a sign of progress, but what is lost when we replace natural foods with modified organisms?

Here it's clear the contrast is between the benefits and drawbacks of progress. Once you isolate the contrast, you're ready to parse the prompt.

Using the simple T-chart introduced in the previous paragraph, we can split the general introduction of this GMO prompt into pro and con arguments. For example:

| Pro | Con |
| --- | --- |
| GMOs are a sign of progress and efficiency. | What is lost when we replace natural foods with modified organisms? |

Now use these contrasting themes to organize the sub-arguments of your essay.

| Sub-arguments | |
| --- | --- |
| GMOs raise food production by increasing crop yields | Movie "Food Inc." exposes negative aspects of GMO |
| Make food more nutritious and resistant to harmful bacteria | Large corporations like Monsanto secretly tampering with food |

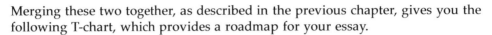

Merging these two together, as described in the previous chapter, gives you the following T-chart, which provides a roadmap for your essay.

| Pro | Con |
|---|---|
| GMOs are a sign of progress and efficiency | What is lost when we replace natural foods with modified organisms? |
| **Sub-arguments** | **Sub-arguments** |
| GMOs raise food production by increasing crop yields | Movie "Food Inc." exposes negative aspects of GMO |
| Make food more nutritious and resistant to harmful bacteria | Large corporations like Monsanto secretly tampering with food |

As in the previous chapter, notice that while some of the sub-arguments are drawn directly from the prompt, others are either extrapolations of the theme (GMOs increase crop yields) or imaginative images from movies ("Food, Inc.") that can be used to add details and depth to the presentation.

You need to use your imagination here in order to come up with interesting arguments you can use in your essay. You have 40 minutes to write the essay so it's OK to spend a little time brainstorming on your pro and con positions.

You'll also want to consider the three perspectives provided by the ACT for each prompt to determine whether you agree or disagree. Remember, as you consider the perspectives, it's important to think of concrete examples you can use to support your case. The devil is always in the details. The more specific examples you provide to buttress your arguments, the higher your essay score.

The point of all these T-charts and all this pre-planning is to help you organize your essay in a clear and straightforward manner with enough concrete detail to impress the ACT readers with the logic, depth and order of your presentation. The point being, of course, to construct a top-scoring essay.

Here's the Perspectives-chart that summarizes the perspectives and provides concrete examples for support:

| Perspectives Chart |
| --- |
| **Perspective One**<br>Lose basic understanding of what we eat. Consumers don't know what they're buying<br><br>CONCRETE EXAMPLES:<br>Companies aren't required to label GMOs - staple foods like corn are injected with insecticide but sold unlabeled<br><br>**Perspective Two**<br>GMOs boost the quality and quantity of our food and, therefore, make the world more prosperous<br><br>CONCRETE EXAMPLES: Apples with high antioxidant content of blueberries, thrive in arid climates<br><br>**Perspective Three**<br>GMOs offer a future of unimagined possibilities for both researchers and consumers<br><br>CONCRETE EXAMPLES: GMOs offer a way to feed growing population but could lead to health problems. Support both pro and con positions. |

This parsing of the prompt and evaluation of perspectives should take you no more than 5 to 10 minutes, after which you'll have a rough outline/roadmap for your essay.

Feel free, of course, to vary or augment the outline as new ideas emerge in the process of writing your essay. This roadmap will ensure that you get to your ultimate destination without being hopelessly sidetracked along the way.

Now let's take a look at another sample essay constructed around the T-charts and Perspectives-chart discussed above. Brandon, one of my top students, agreed to tackle the essay.

# Sample Essay

*Genetically Modified Foods*

The way in which our food is grown has become a hot-button issue. Many people feel that natural farm-made products are superior to artificial ones associated with the rapidly growing industry of genetically modified foods (GMOs). Scientists are using biotechnology to craft and design so-called super-foods that are more nutritious and pest-resistant than their natural counterparts. However, genetic modification remains a controversial subject. Human-based agriculture has existed for thousands of years. What happens to our health and well-being when the human component is reshaped and altered by biotechnology?

In today's society, consumers are more wary than ever about what they are eating. Shoppers rely on nutrition labels to guide them towards healthy choices and away from processed garbage. But what if these labels were hiding something? Surprisingly, food companies aren't required to inform the consumer that their products contain genetically modified organisms. Therefore, staple foods like corn may be injected with harsh insecticides and masquerade as traditional products, rendering the consumer completely unaware as to what they are actually buying. In the viral documentary, "Food Inc.", it is revealed that monopolistic corporations like Monsanto are responsible for this secret genetic tampering. Some critics call these GMO products "franken-food" since they are artificially designed and exist outside of nature.

However, genetically modified food may not be the devil that some make it out to be. From a societal perspective, GMOs offer a way to boost crop yields and feed the world's ever-burgeoning population. Furthermore, these modified crops can be designed to thrive in harsh winters and arid climates where farming was previously impossible. Not to mention these foods can have increased nutrition content. Imagine eating an apple with the high antioxidant content of a blueberry. Soon, parents may be encouraging their kids to eat their GMO fruits and vegetables.

In the timeline of human farming, GMOs are a relatively recent phenomenon. Since their introduction in 1980, the very definition of food has changed. What were once genetically limited crops are now dynamic and customizable plants that can adapt to the needs of our growing population. By eliminating harmful pesticides that pollute groundwater and harm wildlife, ecosystems may be saved and farmlands restored. However, it may turn out that we end up substituting one sort of dangerous compound for another. Laboratory rats exposed to GMO foods, for example, have been know to come down with cancer and a host of other neurological disorders. Many challenges lie ahead.

Overall, the addition of GMOs to our society is a double-edged sword. On one hand, it offers a promising way to solve the world's disastrous hunger problem by both boosting the yield and nutrition of crops. On the other hand, its long-term health ramifications are unknown. The general population serves as unknowing test subjects to this grand experiment of genetic modification. Will GMOs save the world, or be the downfall of humanity? Only time will answer this burning question.

## Building Blocks

As we saw in the previous chapter, every ACT essay is really just a series of building blocks stacked one on top of the other. In this section, we walk through the sample essay from start to finish, highlighting the function of each of the major building blocks.

### Introductory Paragraph

Notice how the introduction of the essay sets the scene by *isolating the contrast* in the second sentence — the conflict between farm-made products and artificial, genetically modified foods. Some of the advantages of GMOs are introduced along with a cautionary, rhetorical question that asks the reader to consider the human downside and potential drawbacks to the technology.

As mentioned previously, rhetorical questions are a sophisticated way for writers to get their points across by inviting the reader to engage directly in the conversation.

### First Body Paragraph

The first body paragraph of the essay supports Perspective One by expanding on the idea that biotechnology companies aren't required to inform the consumer that their products are GMO. More detail is provided about harsh insecticides and the dangers of monopolistic companies like Monsanto. The paragraph concludes with a reference to a popular documentary "Food, Inc." which exposes the evils of so-called "franken-foods." All this provides good supporting detail for the fact that consumers don't actually understand what they're buying when they purchase these modified goods.

### Second Body Paragraph

The second body paragraph takes the opposite position, addressing Perspective Two by arguing that GMOs may offer a way to boost crop yields and feed the world's ever-burgeoning population. This acts as a CONCESSION paragraph to show the writer understands how to evaluate both sides of an argument.

Increased nutritional content and the ability to thrive in arid climates are mentioned as positive qualities of GMOs. A concrete example is given of apples that might possess the same high antioxidant content of blueberries. This is good, imaginative, supporting detail.

### Third Body Paragraph

The third body paragraph, which addresses Perspective Three, presents a mixed bag of arguments both in support of and in opposition to GMOs. Details about health issues like cancer are set against the restoration of farmlands and ecosystems.

### Conclusion

The essay concludes with a summary of the pro and con positions stated throughout the work and ends with a flourish, asking the reader to ponder whether GMOs will save the world or be the downfall of humanity? Nice apocalyptic flourish at the end.

It should be noted, although it may already be abundantly clear, that the conclusion of an ACT essay is really the easiest part. Just roll back through the pro and con arguments you've previously presented in your essay, cherry-picking the best and brightest. Then end with a flourish in the form of a quote, an anecdote, or, as in this case, a rhetorical question about the future of humanity!

### Parting Thoughts

Since this chapter is about variations on a theme, I want to present a different, more imaginative introduction to the essay we just reviewed. Brandon, in fact, wrote two different introductions, the one we just saw, which was good, and another, more imaginative one, which is great.

Lest I give you the impression that your ACT essays have to be all button-down, academic exercises in form and function, let me show you a more adventurous take on an opening salvo for your essay.

*New Intro*

> One year at Thanksgiving, my grandfather jokingly said, "Life expectancy would grow by leaps and bounds if green vegetables smelled as good as bacon." Everybody at the table laughed and agreed wholeheartedly, thinking his joke had no real-life implications. However, thanks to the rapid growth of the GMO industry, his fantasy may soon become reality. Scientists are using biotechnology to craft and design artificial foods that are more nutritious and pest-resistant than their natural counterparts. However, genetic modification remains a controversial subject due to its experimental and artificial nature.

As you can probably agree, this sort of introduction is more tasty, more enticing to the reader than the conventional intro we saw. Of course, it takes a leap of imagination to get off to a cinematic start like this. But if you have the inclination and the stylistic moves to pull this off, my advice is: go for it!

## Return to Intelligent Machines

Finally, since we're talking variations on a theme here, let's return to the sample essay on *Intelligent Machines* from the previous chapter. Here are two different takes on that prompt, one world class, and the other somewhat lacking in both style and substance.

### Caie's Essay

The first variation on the *Intelligent Machines* prompt is by my former student Caie, who constructs such sophisticated, detailed and provocative prose that it's no wonder she got into Harvard!

Intelligent Machines

Twenty years ago, Michael J. Sandel, a leading political philosopher in America, postulated that if we did not place limits on the technological machines that were at the time just beginning to dominate modern society, we would lose our own humanity. For many, his concerns felt unwarranted, because the changes that accompanied these machines meant progress and better communication. Today's reality, however, may lie somewhere between the two extremes: neither fearing these intelligent machines nor praising them unconditionally paints a clear picture of how they should be viewed. Instead, we must acknowledge the labor saving uses of machines while we also realize that their presence can damage our ability to communicate with each other.

It may be argued that because computers are capable of nearly every basic human function, their resource should be utilized for efficiency. Failing to take advantage of progress is not progress at all, as Erik Brynjolfsson explains in The Second Machine Age: computers are now able to pick stocks, diagnose disease, and even grant parole based on analysis of the law. If we have the technology to do work for us – if Google can create a car that drives safer than humans, if programmers can create a Consumer Price Index that updates daily on its own, if machines can track our symptoms better than a trained medical specialist in the field – why shouldn't it be allowed to do so? Having robots that create greater safety and knowledge about humanity augments, not hurts, our own decisions.

But if machines are allowed to do so much, what have we left to their mercy? Although technology may challenge our long-standing ideas about what humans can be, viewing this as an entirely positive phenomenon is to forget its negative consequences. In the past thirty years, what was once only a personal computer became tablets, smartphones, and the cloud. Yet these progressive movements accompanied accelerating income inequality, where highly skilled workers benefited from the changes while leaving huge masses of people behind. Intelligent machines segmented the population into two large groups: those at the top and those at the bottom, leading to an ever-shrinking middle class. These concerns are reflected in much of modern media, with recent titles like, "What Machines Can't Do", "The Robots are Winning", and "More Jobs Predicted for Machines, Not People". Thus, celebrating one side of progress without acknowledging the other is not the way to proceed, either.

So perhaps the answer to the modern place for intelligent machines lies in between: it is time for humanity to find a role that does not create dependency on robots but also allows them to be placed where they function best. It is true that machines are better at low-skill, repetitive jobs, and finding use for them in these places is not a bad thing because everyone benefits from greater efficiency.

However, allowing machines to replace our everyday interactions, as we have already done through mediums like Facebook, Snapchat, or Instagram, may be going too far. Intelligent machines may shift our views about the role of humanity, but they should not eliminate our duties altogether. In the face of ever-increasing routinized information processing, our role is to be passionate, personalized, and far from neutral, for pure emotions like empathy and love cannot be mimicked on a screen. As we continue to move forward in these coming ages of ever-increasing machine capability, it is crucial that we hold on to the emotive, communicative piece of ourselves that will always be able to embody what it means to be human better than a robot.

## Richard's Essay

Now compare and contrast Caie's essay with this offering from Richard, another student of mine who, in an early draft of his essay, is still struggling to find his voice, particularly when it comes to providing concrete details.

**Note:** It's often just as valuable to analyze what went wrong with an essay as it is to applaud what went right!

### Intelligent Machines

In this growing technological age, the use of machines has changed the way we as humans interact with each other. Before the women's rights movement, housewives were bound to their duties of cleaning the house. But with the innovation of household appliances, women were able to spend more time thinking about the status quo of their rights and pushed themselves to gain the unimaginable before their time: the right to vote. With the increased efficiency of intelligent machines comes the price of losing the vital connections between individuals. I personally support the efficiency that intelligent machines can provide us with and believe machines and humans can work together.

Efficiency of machines frees up the time for humans to think of innovative ways to progress humanity. Without the constant burden of working to support a family, humans have more time to think of ways to socially advance themselves. It also gives humans leverage to demand change without the risk of losing the means to feed their family. Ultimately, without the creation of machines, humanity would lack the time to push for progress.

That being said, I do not believe that machines should take away personal interactions. Human interactions should not be replaced by machine services. Looking back on the history of humanity, groups were instinctively formed to create bonds to survive. Therefore, it is not in humanity's best interest to have machines replace the connections that have caused for our success as a species.

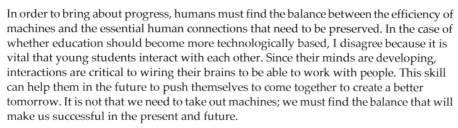

In order to bring about progress, humans must find the balance between the efficiency of machines and the essential human connections that need to be preserved. In the case of whether education should become more technologically based, I disagree because it is vital that young students interact with each other. Since their minds are developing, interactions are critical to wiring their brains to be able to work with people. This skill can help them in the future to push themselves to come together to create a better tomorrow. It is not that we need to take out machines; we must find the balance that will make us successful in the present and future.

The development of intelligent machines speaks to humans astonishing ability to think and improve our lives. It is our job now to adapt the role machines play in our lives to progress humanity toward a future of endless possibilities while maintaining our own humanity.

Several problems should be apparent to you at once in this essay. Let's break the writing down paragraph by paragraph.

First of all, the introductory paragraph is "fuzzy"; which is to say it lacks clarity, cohesion and contrasts. The writer rambles on about women's rights, housework, the status quo and the right to vote. What these topics have to do with intelligent machines is not specifically clear. Richard unwisely addresses the prompt with abstractions that skirt the topic rather than illuminate it.

When he finally gets to the meat of the matter — the contrasts explicit in the prompt — he offers a fairly bland summary:

> With the increased efficiency of intelligent machines comes the price of losing the vital connections between individuals.

Compare this with Caie's introduction, where the contrasting aspects of the prompt are clearly delineated:

> Today's reality, however, may lie somewhere between the two extremes: neither fearing these intelligent machines nor praising them unconditionally paints a clear picture of how they should be viewed.

To make matters worse, Richard turns the focus on himself in the last sentence of the paragraph, saying:

> I personally support the efficiency that intelligent machines can provide us with and believe machines and humans can work together.

Well, truth be told, the ACT readers don't really care what he *believes* unless he can buttress his belief with concrete examples that relate directly to the prompt. Vague personal pronouncements won't cut it.

Compare the end of Richards intro paragraph to the final sentence of Caie's introduction, where she says:

Instead, we must acknowledge the labor saving uses of machines while we also realize that their presence can damage our ability to communicate with each other.

Using "we", as Caie does, rather than "I", as Richard does, draws the reader into the writing and implies that the writer will take an objective — rather than subjective — stand on the issues.

ACT readers are looking for analysis of the prompt and support for positions taken, *not* personal opinions!

In the next paragraph, Richard mentions that:

Efficiency of machines frees up the time for humans to think of innovative ways to progress humanity.

What's missing here are concrete details, specific examples that demonstrate HOW machines free up time for humans to become more innovative.

Caie, in contrast, fills her second paragraph with interesting details like these:

Computers are now able to pick stocks, diagnose disease, and even grant parole based on analysis of the law . . . we have the technology do work for us – if Google can create a car that drives safer than humans, if programmers can create a Consumer Price Index . . .

And so on. For good writers, the devil is in the details, details, details.

In the third paragraph, Richard starts to make progress: he introduces a concession to the prompt — an essential part of every ACT essay — but follows that with a series of bland pronouncements, writing:

That being said, I do not believe that machines should take away personal interactions. Human interactions should not be replaced by machine services. Looking back on the history of humanity, groups were instinctively formed to create bonds to survive. Therefore, it is not in humanity's best interest to have machines replace the connections that have caused for our success as a species.

Finally, his conclusion is weak since it doesn't summarize the contrasts of the prompt or the perspectives provided. Compare it to Caie's essay where major points are recapped, new details are provided and an inspiring conclusion is broached.

Not to pile on but one final point: Richard's overall word count is low, barely reaching 400 words. Top-scoring ACT essays clock in at 450 or more words.

### Last Word

On some level, of course, it's not fair to directly compare a world-class essay with one less accomplished. Still, showing how it should be done can help illuminate how it could be done for students struggling to improve their prose.

To paraphrase the great Spanish philosopher, Santayana: "Those who don't understand their mistakes are forever forced to repeat them."

With this in mind, then, let's recap the main mistakes in Richard's essay:

1. A rambling unfocused introductory paragraph that fails to parse the prompt and isolate the contrast

2. A subjective, rather than objective, analysis of the topic

3. A tendency to write in bland abstract pronouncements

4. A lack of concrete supporting detail throughout the essay

5. A weak conclusion that fails to summarize the perspectives provided and the contrasting points of view

6. An essay deficient in word count

## What's Next

After you've written an essay, it helps to know how to score it. In the next chapter we'll delve into the rubric (rules) that ACT readers are expected to apply when scoring essays. I'll also give my take on the rubric in order to bring it down to earth.

# 5—Scoring ACT Essays

The ACT has provided a rubric for use in scoring the essay. In this chapter, I'll first present the "official" version of how ACT readers are instructed to score essays; then I'll cut through the verbiage and translate the "official" scoring rubric into more digestible, easy-to-assimilate terms.

## ACT Scoring Guidelines

The full and complete ACT scoring guidelines are available for viewing on the ACT website. If you're a glutton for punishment and interested in plowing through the complete list, you can find them at:

http://www.act.org/writing/scores/guidelines.html

Thankfully, the ACT had the good sense to subdivide the rubric into four reasonably clear subsections. Here are the four overarching criteria.

- Ideas and Analysis
- Development and Support
- Organization
- Language Use and Convention

Text from the ACT defining each subsection is given below, followed by my translation.

### Ideas and Analysis

*Official ACT Scoring Rubric* — Scores in this domain reflect the ability to generate productive ideas and engage critically with multiple perspectives on the given issue. Competent writers understand the issue they are invited to address, the purpose for writing, and the audience. They generate ideas that are relevant to the situation.

*What This Really Means* —Writers must be able to parse the prompt, interpret the perspectives, and express ideas relevant to the topic at hand, preferably with nuance and complexity.

## Development and Support

*Official ACT Scoring Rubric* — Scores in this domain reflect the ability to discuss ideas, offer rationale, and bolster an argument. Competent writers explain and explore their ideas, discuss implications, and illustrate through examples. They help the reader understand their thinking about the issue.

*What This Really Means* — A well-developed, persuasive essay argues pro or con positions concerning the perspectives in a cohesive, logical and integrated manner. Arguments with well-defined, concrete examples should be employed to support your positions. Don't argue opinions; instead, argue facts.

## Organization

*Official ACT Scoring Rubric* — Scores in this domain reflect the ability to organize ideas with clarity and purpose. Organizational choices are integral to effective writing. Competent writers arrange their essay in a way that clearly shows the relationship between ideas, and they guide the reader through their discussion.

*What This Really Means* — Writers must organize their essays around a classic structure: an intro, 2 or more body paragraphs, and a conclusion. The into should establish context for the general topic, employing quotes, anecdotes or citations. Subsequently, the prompt should be parsed into clear pro and con positions. Writers can either take a stand on the prompt in their intro or wait until later to take sides.

The body paragraphs should address the perspectives with logical arguments and concrete examples. Don't jump from one paragraph to the next. Use clear transitions *between* paragraphs. Glide. Transitions guide readers through your arguments in a logical and straightforward manner.

Your conclusion should summarize the positions taken and should end with a flourish. It's OK to fold arguments for a perspective into your conclusion. Bonus points for adding another quote or anecdote to give further and final context to your conclusion.

## Language Use and Conventions

*Official ACT Scoring Rubric* — Scores in this domain reflect the ability to use written language to convey arguments with clarity. Competent writers make use of the conventions of grammar, syntax, word usage, and mechanics. They are also aware of their audience and adjust the style and tone of their writing to communicate effectively.

*What This Really Means* — Writers must employ sentence variety, transitions *within* paragraphs, flash vocab and details, details, details in their essays. See my "Rules of Engagement" in Chapter 2 for a complete list of language use and conventions.

**Note:** I find it ironic that ACT uses such abstract terminology in its rubric when ACT essays will be graded on the ability of writers to make pragmatic, persuasive and fact-based analysis of the issues presented.

One last thought: although the ACT powers-that-be never say so directly, a concession paragraph is essential for a top-scoring essay since it shows "flexibility of thought processing" and the ability to "balance both sides of an argument." Be sure to include a concession paragraph in your essay. However, as I mention in Chapter 3, it's easy to include a concession paragraph since the prompt and perspectives are built around contrasting points of view.

≡

# My Take

Having boiled this rubric down to terms that we can all understand, let me summarize the major points of interest that I look for in a top-scoring essay.

1. An intro that provides broad context for the thesis at hand. Could be in the form of quotes or anecdotes or both. Fluid writing style and interesting sentence structure: subordination, transitions, vocab.

2. An intro, once context has been established, that parses the prompt into pro and con positions and clearly isolates the contrasts.

3. Body paragraphs that address each of the three perspectives provided by the ACT. Writers may include two perspectives in one paragraph, fold one of the perspectives into the conclusion or handle perspectives one by one in separate paragraphs. The key point is for writers to support their take on each perspective with *details, details, details*. No wishy-washy sentences like "I feel that . . ." or "My considered opinion would be . . . ". If it's *just* an opinion, it's not "considered."

   In Chapter 6, "Other Essays", we'll take a look at sample essays from my students, some of whom take the straightforward "one perspective per paragraph" approach. Others may use a less formulaic approach, blending perspectives in multiple paragraphs or using two or more paragraphs on a single perspective. Dealer's choice.

4. Writing that shows imagination and intelligence. This one is harder to quantify. More of an art than a science.

5. Effective use of *both* kinds of transitions — transitions between paragraphs and transitions within paragraphs. See Chapter 2 "Rules of Engagement" for more detail.

6. A conclusion that summarizes positions and provides final context, putting the contrasting points of view into perspective.

7. Overall, I look for persuasive arguments, logical progression, narrative cohesion, and writer's point of view, which includes style, tone and analysis.

Of course, you rarely see an essay that has all of these components, but the more the better.

## Dos and Dont's

Not to gild the lily here, but some students might think that even the list above is too abstract. So, in the spirit of complete egalitarianism, I'll post a series of Do's and Dont's for the very literal minded.

- Do write an essay with a clear beginning, middle and end. Plan your essay carefully before you start to write. Chart a well-organized course. Don't just start writing without a roadmap or outline. Don't bluff. Don't front.

- Do take a strong position on the prompt and maintain logical focus throughout. Don't ramble. Don't waffle. Stay on target.

- Do consider both pro and con arguments. Don't just side with one perspective and neglect the other(s). Remember to provide a concession paragraph.

- Do be specific. The more concrete examples cited the better. Don't write in vague generalities. Don't make wishy-washy statements like this: "In my opinion the prompt discusses several points of view and all of them should be addressed, which I plan to do in my essay."

- Do use transitions between and within paragraphs to guide the reader in a logical fashion through the essay. Don't jump haphazardly from one paragraph to the next, neglecting narrative cohesion. Don't crash and burn.

- Do use a variety of sentence structures, including subordination, when presenting your arguments. Don't write in short, choppy sentences that have no flow and won't go.

Essays receiving low scores are deficient in one or more of these criteria.

## What's Next

In the next chapter, "Other Essays," we'll examine several sample essays written by my students to give you a more concrete idea of how to put these rules into practice to create a top-scoring essay. All the sample essays are presented with T-charts and Perspectives-charts to provide a clear methodology.

# 6—Other Essays

Most people agree, practice makes perfect. In that spirit, this chapter presents several sample essays written by various students of mine to address a variety of prompts and perspectives. These essays, complete with T-charts and Perspective Charts, reinforce and compliment the methodology presented in previous chapters.

After reading through this chapter, you should come away with a solid grasp of ACT essay mechanics.

All essays mirror the format provided by the ACT and are written by various students of mine. After each essay, I provide comments and reprise tidbits of the ACT scoring rubric from the previous chapter.

Here are the topics covered:

- Gender Gap
- Concerns over Developmental Biology
- Photo Sharing on Social Media
- Impact of Commercial Television
- Different Sides of Multitasking

# Gender Gap

The role that gender plays in financial and social relationships has been studied and discussed for decades now. In this sample essay, one of my brightest students, Millie, tackles the issues head on.

**Sample Prompt**

*Gender Gap*

The role of men and women in society has long been debated. Some recent findings in sociology suggest that gender plays an important role in both financial activities and social relationships. In one experiment, called the "Dictator Game", women were found to be more generous than men. Male and female players were given a set amount of money and allowed — but not required — to distribute various amounts to hidden and anonymous partners. At the end of the game, it was determined that women gave away twice as much money as men. In yet another game, women were seen as quite willing to compete against other women but much less willing to compete against men.

*Read and carefully consider these perspectives. Each suggests a particular way of thinking about the issues of gender identity.*

| Perspective One | Perspective Two | Perspective Three |
|---|---|---|
| In economic activities, men are perceived as dominant players. They take stronger negotiating positions in financial matters. They may be "stingy" compared to women, but this trait makes them better able to control the bottom line. | Women should not be viewed as "softies" who are willing to settle for less. This is a distortion of gender and talent. Women are by nature more social than men. Consequently, they are more apt to work for the good of the group rather than that of the individual. | Women and men both have roles to play in the financial community. But these roles are not fixed by gender. Individuals should not be stereotyped but allowed to play to their respective strengths, whatever those may be. |

<table>
<tr><td colspan="1" align="center">Essay Task</td></tr>
</table>

| **Essay Task** |
| --- |
| Write a unified, coherent essay in which you evaluate multiple perspectives on the concerns expressed regarding gender identity. In your essay, be sure to:<br><br>• analyze and evaluate the perspectives given<br><br>• state and develop your own perspective on the issue<br><br>• explain the relationship between your perspective and those given<br><br>Your perspective may be in full agreement with any of the others, in partial agreement, or wholly different. Whatever the case, support your ideas with logical reasoning and detailed, persuasive examples. |

### Isolate the Contrast

As usual, the prompt provides clear-cut pro and con positions on the topic, which you can cherry pick to get your essay started. Use a T-chart to state your positions and organize your sub-arguments. For example:

| **Pro** | **Con** |
| --- | --- |
| Gender plays an important role in financial activities and social relationships | People's roles in the economy and society shouldn't be defined based off of gender |

Sub-arguments

| | |
| --- | --- |
| Studies have shown that men aren't as generous in financial matters but play the more dominant role | Men and women are both equally capable of having strengths in all areas despite gender (ex. Rosalind Franklin, Bill Gates) |
| Women are more social than men and therefore work better in groups — Marissa Mayer of Google | Statistical evidence shows that women can play a dominant role in stereotypical male jobs (ex. Math, CEO) |
| Use personal experience to show the influence of gender in the family | Men can also be humanitarians — MLK |

**Perspectives**

The main point of each of the perspectives provided is summarized below and concrete examples are attached to support various positions. For example:

<table>
<tr><td align="center">Perspectives Chart</td></tr>
<tr><td>

**Perspective 1**
Men are the dominant players in economic activities.

CONCRETE EXAMPLES: Kids look to the head of the household, generally the male figure, for money. Majority of women generally didn't work until after WWII which is what has caused the economic discrepancy between the genders.

**Perspective 2**
Women are social and willing to work for the good of the group.

CONCRETE EXAMPLES: Marissa Mayer, senior executive for Google, shows how women, who have the ability to collaborate well with others, can play an important part in the economy.

**Perspective 3**
You can't define the role people play in financial and social matters based on gender.

CONCRETE EXAMPLES: Statistical evidence of women being involved in math, female scientists such as Rosalind Franklin, and male humanitarians such as Bill Gates, Martin Luther King Jr., etc.

</td></tr>
</table>

Remember that this chart is simply a means to organize the way you want to handle each of the given perspectives. Once you've mapped out your general arguments, feel free to enlarge upon your positions, add alternate explanations or introduce new concrete examples. The chart is a springboard to get you rolling on your essay.

## Sample Essay

*Gender Gap*

As the 21st Century has progressed, the debate over gender inequality has been a controversial topic making news headlines all over the country and furthermore, the world. Emma Watson, the UN ambassador for the "He for She" campaign, turned heads when she gave her speech on gender inequality in 2014. With the controversy over the disparity between the sexes becoming increasingly pronounced, people have taken to scientific tests to examine the fundamental interactions among men and women, often reaching the conclusion that women are generally more generous to others however less assertive when interacting with men. Men are therefore seen as the more dominant and controlling figures. However, women are often more social than men and are more likely to work for the good of the group, rather than just for themselves. Although there is no definite answer in the debate over gender, it is important to consider the role gender plays in financial and social interactions.

When looking to economic activities, men clearly play the dominant role in financial matters giving them the capability to have the final say. As a child of two doctors, I have been witness to the work both of my parents do and the roughly equal paycheck that they receive at the end of the month. However, the ingrained idea that the male is the head of the household had taught me, unknowingly, to look to my father as my source of revenue when I needed money for a movie or any other leisure activity. And from my observations over the years, I know that I am not alone in this behavior. It wasn't until after Word War II that women were truly allowed to become active members in the workforce. Men have historically been the dominant bread winners.

However, women are more social by nature and work more for the good of the group, allowing for the prosperity of the work force while helping to invalidate the claim that women are "softies". For example, one of the senior executives for Google is Marissa Mayer, whose collaboration with fellow coworkers and innovative ideas have changed how people all over the world get information on the Internet. By exchanging ideas with other members of Google rather than simply working alone, Mayer played a pivotal role in fostering the immense success of the search engine that is so commonplace today.

Although it is easy to try and segregate people based on gender, there is no way to truly define differences between men or women based on economic or social factors. According to the Washington Post, women make up for more than 40 percent of the degrees in statistics. Similarly, it is seen throughout history that women and men can defy the typical view of gender roles. Rosalind Franklin, a scientist during the 1930's and 1940's was the first person to take a picture of DNA using x-ray crystallography that allowed people to uncover the double helix shape of DNA. Working against all sorts of discrimination based on her sex, she is an example of how we can't constrain people in social and economic straight-jackets. In addition, famous male humanitarians include Mahatma Gandhi, Martin Luther King Jr., Bill Gates, and a plethora of others. It is imperative that people, despite their gender, be given the freedom and encouragement to pursue their own interests without being influenced by stereotypes.

It is clear that there is a wide array of views on the differences between genders. While studies have shown that men are generally the more dominant and stringent group, females are also more social and selfless. However, there is no way to try and polarize both sexes into opposing groups without harming the strengths of the human race, despite their gender. Only as time goes on and gender perceptions continue to evolve we will be able to see how the chips fall.

## Comments

Notice how Millie sets the stage for her essay with a reference to Emma Watson's speech on gender equality. Starting your essay off with a quote, anecdote or historical reference gets the immediate attention of the reader. She follows this up by citing the pro and can positions presented in the prompt.

In the following paragraph, Millie uses personal experience to flesh out the first Perspective 1, showing how family dynamics and historical events can overtly influence gender identity. By making the topic personal, Millie avoids getting lost in abstract pronouncements. Instead, she gives concrete details from her childhood and adolescence.

In contrast to the emphasis on male dominance conveyed in the previous paragraph, Millie addresses Perspective Two in her next body paragraph by emphasizing the collaborative nature of women in the workplace, using Marissa Mayer as an example of a high-achieving collaborator. She gives important details of her work with Google.

Perspective Three is actually used as a "concession" paragraph since it announces that there is no way to truly define gender differences. The paragraph then presents examples of women working individually in science and men working socially in humanitarian endeavors. This paragraph turns the tables on the prompt by showing examples that defy gender stereotypes. The concluding paragraph sums up the various pro and con positions of the prompt and ends by advising that gender perceptions are an evolving aspect of social relations.

## ACT Rubric in a Nutshell

To boil the ACT rubric down to its essentials, ask yourself the following questions:

- Does the essay express ideas and analysis relevant to the prompt?
- Does the essay make a well-developed, well-supported argument for the various positions and perspectives?
- Is the essay organized in such a way as to lead the reader through the arguments in a logical and persuasive manner?
- Does the writer employ sentence variety, use transitions and supply sufficient detail to convey arguments with clarity and conviction?

Think of these questions as a mini-rubric that you should apply not only to the essays in this chapter but to your own writing as well. I leave the answers up to you, knowing that if you can say "yes" to these criteria, you are well on your way to composing a top-scoring essay of your own.

# Concerns over Developmental Biology

Genetic screening tests can provoke both hope and consternation for parents-to-be. In this essay, Grace, another student of mine, does a terrific job of painting both sides of the issue.

**Sample Prompt**

*Concerns over Developmental Biology*

Technological progress in the field of developmental biology has allowed scientists to conduct what is known as genetic diagnosis, where, by taking tissue samples of individuals before birth, a child may be characterized through the analysis of particular genes. Parents, in other words, may be able to know not only the most obvious genetic malfunctions of their child before birth, but also the full range of genetic possibilities their baby possesses. Though this progress allows for greater information, there is also some concern about the darker implications of the technology. What are the risks of knowing the complete genetic makeup of a child before it is born? Given the growing popularity of these tests, it is worth considering the long-term implications of genetic diagnosis.

*Read and carefully consider these perspectives. Each suggests a particular way of thinking about the effects of genetic testing.*

| Perspective One | Perspective Two | Perspective Three |
| --- | --- | --- |
| Screening tests can help parents-to-be know whether the fetus is at high risk for a chromosomal abnormality, allowing for better planning and preparation. | Pre-birth knowledge about the condition of the fetus could lead to conflicting emotions for parents. Knowing the genetic risks diminishes some of the joy and expectancy of the experience. | Even with increased technology, screening tests do not always lend themselves to accurate information. Birth defects can occur at any point during pregnancy. |

---

┌─────────────────────────────────────────────────────────────┐
│                       **Essay Task**                        │
├─────────────────────────────────────────────────────────────┤
│ Write a unified, coherent essay in which you evaluate multiple │
│ perspectives on the concerns over genetic screening. In your essay, be │
│ sure to:                                                     │
│                                                              │
│  • analyze and evaluate the perspectives given              │
│                                                              │
│  • state and develop your own perspective on the issue      │
│                                                              │
│  • explain the relationship between your perspective and    │
│    those given                                              │
│                                                              │
│ Your perspective may be in full agreement with any of the others, in │
│ partial agreement, or wholly different. Whatever the case, support │
│ your ideas with logical reasoning and detailed, persuasive examples. │
└─────────────────────────────────────────────────────────────┘

## Isolate the Contrast

As usual, the prompt provides clear-cut pro and con positions on the topic, which you can cherry pick to get your essay started. Use a T-chart to state your positions and organize your sub-arguments. For example:

| Pro | Con |
|---|---|
| Screening tests give parents-to-be more information about their unborn baby | More information can diminish the joy in the "miracle of life" for parents |

### Sub-arguments

| | |
|---|---|
| Parents can prepare financially or emotionally to support their child | Screening tests are not always accurate and can be wrong |
| With more information about their child's physical disabilities, parents are better prepared to terminate the pregnancy | Stacie and Lincoln Chapman almost terminated their pregnancy, but ended up having a healthy baby |

**Perspectives**

Now address the main point of each of the perspectives provided below the prompt and attach concrete examples to support your positions. For example:

<table>
<tr><td align="center">Perspectives Chart</td></tr>
<tr><td>

**Perspective 1**
Screening tests are good and can help parents plan ahead if their child is born with a birth defect, or the parents can make other arrangements.

CONCRETE EXAMPLES: Medical bills for birth defects cost the US billions annually, and parents must plan ahead financially or make other arrangements for the child or the pregnancy.

**Perspective 2**
Screening tests lower the happiness that comes along with pregnancy.

CONCRETE EXAMPLES:
Parental stress due to knowledge of diseases such as Down's Syndrome.

**Perspective 3**
Screening tests are not infallible. Birth defects are not always apparent until late in pregnancy.

CONCRETE EXAMPLES: Plight of Stacy and Lincoln Chapman, parents who went against their doctor's advice.

</td></tr>
</table>

Remember: this chart is simply a means to organize the way you want to handle each of the given perspectives. Once you've mapped out your general arguments, feel free to enlarge upon your positions, add alternate explanations or introduce new concrete examples. The chart is a springboard to get you rolling on your essay.

## Sample Essay

*Concerns over Developmental Biology*

Biologist Richard Dawkins once said, "DNA neither cares nor knows. DNA just is. And we dance to its music." DNA determines what we look like and how our bodies work, but sometimes during pregnancies, things can go wrong. Parents are now able to detect if their unborn child is at risk for a birth defect or disease with genetic screenings. However, many parents and doctors fail to weigh in both the positive and negative aspects of the testing. These tests give parents information about their unborn baby, and the knowledge can be either helpful or alarming. Consequently, it is worth considering the long-term implications of genetic diagnosis.

Babies born with diseases or birth defects can, and most likely will, change their parent's lives. In serious cases, the screenings can detect if a baby will be born with a life threatening disease or defect, such as Edward Syndrome, congenital heart defects and more. With certain serious diseases, the baby will not survive for very long after birth; its life span could range from a few weeks, to under two years. These diseases may cause the child pain as well, and what parents want their child to live an extremely short, painful life? Genetic screenings can prevent a child from suffering; if they terminate the pregnancy, the unborn baby does not suffer.

According to the Center for Disease Control, hospitalization for birth defects costs the United States over 2 billion annually. From a financial point of view, birth defects and diseases can cost parents thousands of dollars in medical bills, money that they might not have, and can leave parents and siblings feeling affected by the child's disorder. However, with genetic screening, parents can choose to terminate the pregnancy if they are unable to support a child with birth defects.  But if the parents can support the child financially, genetic screenings can help parents plan ahead for the necessities their child will need, such as caretakers, certain doctors, and in some cases, certain foods. These tests can help parents and babies alike.

On the other hand, genetic screenings can make the "miracle of life" less joyful and more stressful for the parents. Knowing that your child will be born with a disease can be a devastating experience that can affect the whole family. Knowledge that an unborn child has Down's Syndrome, for example, is a difficult burden for parents to bear.

Not only that, but prenatal screenings can be wrong. According to a recent story on NBC news, parents-to-be, Stacie and Lincoln Chapman, were pregnant with their first child, and were advised to take a screening test. After doing so, they were told that their child would most likely be born with Edward's Syndrome and would only live a few weeks. Against their doctor's advice, they made the decision to proceed with the pregnancy. Their child was born happy, healthy, and without defects. Stacie and Lincoln were ecstatic that their child was spared; however, they worried for other parents who might decide to terminate their pregnancy due to a prenatal screening.

Prenatal screenings definitely have pros as well as cons. Parents are able to prepare if their child will be at high risk to be born with a birth defect; however, screening tests do not always give accurate information. Today almost 1 in 33 babies is born with a birth

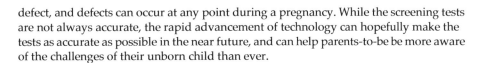

defect, and defects can occur at any point during a pregnancy. While the screening tests are not always accurate, the rapid advancement of technology can hopefully make the tests as accurate as possible in the near future, and can help parents-to-be be more aware of the challenges of their unborn child than ever.

### Comments

Nice opening quote from Richard Dawkins to set the scene. Then Grace parses the prompt into pro and con positions, demonstrating the various ways, positive and negative, that we might "dance to the music."

After parsing the prompt, Grace addresses Perspective 1 (and leads into Perspective 3) by drawing on her sophomore physiology class to cite Edward Syndrome and congenital heart disease as some of the problem areas genetic screening might reveal. She follows this up with a rhetorical question that focuses on the suffering genetic testing might alleviate.

The second body paragraph brings in more concrete detail in the form of statistical data from the CDC concerning birth defects. Grace uses the phrase "From a financial point of view" as a nice framing device and transition for her discussion of monetary problems a child's disorder might bring to parents and siblings.

The third body paragraph acts initially as a concession paragraph, using "On the other hand" to shift the readers attention to one of the drawbacks of genetic testing, providing commentary on Perspective 2. This paragraph is admittedly short; more concrete detail would have been a nice addition.

The following paragraph comments on Perspective 3 by emphasizing the drawbacks of genetic testing. The plight of Lincoln Chapman, drawn from NBC news, is presented to emphasize some of the conflicting emotions genetic testing can engender.

The concluding sentence ends on an ambiguous note, citing both the positive and negative attributes of prenatal screening. The fact that every 1 in 33 babies today is born with a birth defect gives the conclusion poignancy and highlights the challenges facing parents who opt for genetic testing.

### ACT Rubric in a Nutshell

To once again boil the ACT rubric down to its essentials, ask yourself the following questions:

- Does the essay express ideas and analysis relevant to the prompt?
- Does the essay make a well-developed, well-supported argument for the various positions and perspectives?

- Is the essay organized in such a way as to lead the reader through the arguments in a logical and persuasive manner?

- Does the writer employ sentence variety, use transitions and supply sufficient detail to convey arguments with clarity and conviction?

Your answers will illuminate and inform your own essay writing.

# Photo-sharing on Social Media

Social Media is a two-edged sword, both increasing the efficiency of communication and distorting the connections between individuals. Tina, one of my students well-versed in social media herself, covers the pros and cons of the issue in a straightforward and compelling essay.

**Sample Prompt**

*The Effects of Photo-sharing on Social Media*

Many of the activities and entertainment we enjoy daily on our cell phones is supplied by large, data-driven startups and applications. These companies build products that allow us to communicate in photos through our phones, where once there were only direct ways of speaking with each other about our lives. Many of our travels and experiences are now shared not with individual people but with the masses, through sophisticated technologies on applications like Instagram or Snapchat. We can now share a picture-perfect, edited version of ourselves. These mediums of photograph-sharing are generally seen as a sign of progress, but what is lost when we replace memories shared directly and in person with those close to us with filtered images and short, hash-tagged explanations? Given the accelerating variety and prevalence of these apps, it is worth examining the implications and meaning of their presence in our lives.

*Read and carefully consider these perspectives. Each suggests a particular way of thinking about the effects of photo-sharing.*

| Perspective One | Perspective Two | Perspective Three |
|---|---|---|
| What we lose with the replacement of direct conversation about our daily experiences is some part of our ability to truly communicate. Our attempts to obtain more "views" and "likes" on social media distorts the way we represent ourselves. | Photo-sharing apps are good at showing others quick and fleeting pictures that capture moments of our everyday lives. This efficiency leads to a more connected and progressive world for everyone. | Picture-sharing apps challenge our long-standing ideas about what long-distance or shared experiences can mean. Technology is pushing us toward new forms of social interaction. |

＝

---

| Essay Task |
|---|
| Write a unified, coherent essay in which you evaluate multiple perspectives on effects of photo-sharing. In your essay, be sure to:<br><br>• analyze and evaluate the perspectives given<br><br>• state and develop your own perspective on the issue<br><br>• explain the relationship between your perspective and those given<br><br>Your perspective may be in full agreement with any of the others, in partial agreement, or wholly different. Whatever the case, support your ideas with logical reasoning and detailed, persuasive examples. |

## Isolate the Contrast

As usual, the prompt provides clear-cut pro and con positions on the topic, which you can cherry pick to get your essay started. Use a T-chart to state your positions and organize your sub-arguments. For example:

| Pro | Con |
|---|---|
| Photo-sharing apps generate an efficiency that leads to a more connected and progressive world for everyone. | Photo-sharing apps result in loss of ability to truly communicate + find self-fulfillment |
| **Sub-arguments** | |
| Easy and quick way to update people on life events: wedding, graduation, new born, birthday | Genuine conversations replaced... Phone calls stiff and formal, so Snapchat/Instagram preferred |
| Universal method of communication. No words needed. Evokes emotions and memories | A user's dependency on public approval through the quantity of "likes" and "followers" that they have. Inability to determine what makes themselves happy. |

**Perspectives**

Now address the main point of each of the perspectives provided below the prompt and attach concrete examples to support your positions. For example:

| Perspectives Chart |
|---|
| **Perspective 1**<br>Use of photo-sharing apps result in loss of ability to communicate and find self-fulfillment.<br><br>CONCRETE EXAMPLES: I no longer call people because I can merely IG/Snap; Sad when I get few likes on a picture and happy when I get many likes on a picture.<br><br>**Perspective 2**<br>Photo-sharing apps generate an efficiency that leads to a more connected and progressive world for everyone.<br><br>CONCRETE EXAMPLES: Photo-sharing connects people over long distances. Bridal showers, commencement ceremonies, trips to the Bahamas can all be shared instantaneously.<br><br>**Perspective 3**<br>Humans and technology work together towards unimagined possibility<br><br>CONCRETE EXAMPLES: privacy settings (Facebook), location tag settings (IG), vanishing photos/videos (Snapchat) |

Remember, this chart is simply a springboard to get you rolling on your essay. Feel free to vary or augment any of these concrete examples as you move through your essay.

## Sample Essay

*The Effects of Photo-Sharing on Social Media*

According to recent studies in the Wall Street Journal, Americans now spend more time staring at their mobile phones during the day than at televisions. Once serving as simply a means of communication, our cellular devices are now equipped with music, a camera, a navigation system and also apps for games, the news, social media, movies and pretty much anything else you can think of. It's no wonder that our Smartphones have practically become the third arm that humans were never born with. Critics worry that photo-sharing apps replace genuine conversations and create a user's dependency on

63

public approval through the quantity of "likes" and "followers" that they have. While it is essential to acknowledge the downfalls of photo-sharing apps, these revolutionary technological developments have provided us with efficiency in communication, resulting in a more connected and progressive world.

Photo-sharing apps, such as Instagram and Snapchat, undoubtedly provide a casual and instantaneous means of communication. Truth be told, I prefer this method of communication over a phone call, which can be uncomfortable and formal. But, as a result of photo-sharing apps, direct conversation is lost: sharing photos replaces calling someone on the phone and telling them about an experience. Apps like Snapchat and Instagram don't really let people communicate deeply, as conversations are shallow and short-lived, punctuated by a myriad of "likes" and "views"

Furthermore, from a psychological standpoint, photo-sharing apps can result in an inability to live in the moment and find self-fulfilment, as I have experienced personally and have seen among other people my age. When going out with friends to the beach, to the city, or to get food, we often spend the majority of the time taking pictures rather than actually enjoying the environment, and each other's company. In addition, just as many likes on a photo can make me happy, few likes on a photo can make me sad. Photo-sharing apps allow other people to determine one's happiness on trivial exchanges of information and can hinder a person's personal discovery of joy.

In contrast, photo-sharing apps have generated an efficient and universal means of communication that, in a sense, has enhanced our connectedness with the world. In the busy, fast-paced life of the modern human, apps like Instagram provide an easy, instantaneous and visual way for one to communicate and keep others updated, and thus help us maintain diverse and long-distance relationships. A photo of one's bridal shower can inform people of an upcoming marriage, while a photo of someone at their commencement ceremony informs followers of a graduation. Photo-sharing is truly a universal method of communication.

Clearly, photo-sharing apps contain both drawbacks and benefits. Apps like Instagram and Snapchat have been accused of replacing genuine conversations and have been criticized for creating a user's dependency on public approval for happiness. On the other hand, the photo-sharing apps have generated an efficient method of communication that results in a more connected world. As Canadian singer-songwriter Joni Mitchell sings, "Well something's lost but something's gained." Essentially, loss comes with modernization. Yet over time, our technology will keep enhancing the ways of social media. As our world continues to progress technologically, and our previous ideas regarding shared experiences are reinvented, humans and technology may work together, producing new forms of social interaction.

## Comments

Tina gets off to a great start by referencing recent studies regarding mobile phones. It's always good to establish context in your introductory paragraph by citing a study, relating an anecdote, or using a quote. In fact, Tina supplies two quotes later on in her intro, engaging the reader with cinema-like dialogue. This gives her essay drama and immediacy. Having set the scene, she goes on to parse the prompt into pro and con positions. Rather than take an unbiased, objective position on the prompt, like several of our previous student writers have shown, Tina clearly sides with the benefits of technology. This is fine. Whether you decide to stay neutral in the intro or takes sides on the prompt is a matter of personal style.

The second paragraph is told from Tina's personal point of view, a strategy that allows her to address Perspective 1, using details "likes" and "views" to demonstrate shallow communication. Nice vocab, too: myriad.

Tina employs a double transition in the third paragraph, starting off with "furthermore" to show the reader she's continuing on with the same train of thought, followed immediately by "from a psychological standpoint", which enables her to delve a little more deeply into the negative emotional effects photo-sharing apps have on personal relations.

The concession paragraph comes next as Tina addresses Perspective 2 by pointing out the positive side of photo-sharing. Events like bridal showers and commencement ceremonies are beautiful moments that can be captured and shared by friends and family alike.

Finally, Tina folds Perspective 3 into her conclusion by citing the ways humans and technology work together. Notice how she quotes the lyrics to a Joni Mitchell song to emphasize the pros and cons of photo-sharing. The use of song lyrics lends objective and artistic depth to the essay. Moreover, she uses the lyrics as a springboard to summarize the pro and con positions she's discussed throughout her essay. She ends with an upbeat view of humans and technology working together.

≡

## ACT Rubric in a Nutshell

Again, to boil the ACT rubric down to its essentials, ask yourself the following questions:

- Does the essay express ideas and analysis relevant to the prompt?
- Does the essay make a well-developed, well-supported argument for the various positions and perspectives?
- Is the essay organized in such a way as to lead the reader through the arguments in a logical and persuasive manner?
- Does the writer employ sentence variety, use transitions and supply sufficient detail to convey arguments with clarity and conviction?

If your answer to these questions is starting to become second nature, good. Internalize these points and your ACT essays will shine!

# Impact of Commercial Television

The role of television in modern society and the way it shapes and influences cultural norms is a topic of great controversy. For this sample prompt, my student, Caiseen, composes an essay of great complexity and detail.

**Sample Prompt**

*Impact of Commercial Television*

Since the advent of television, cultural critics have debated the effects of TV on youth and its impact on modern society. A French social scientist went so far as to say, "Commercial television makes you stupid". He cited a decline in critical analysis among American television watchers due to the lack of educational programming and the ubiquitous presence of commercial advertising. Not all critics agree, however. Many point to evening news and documentaries that provide a window into American society and enlighten viewers on the cultural, political, and social issues of the day. Given these diverse views on television, it's worth examining the meaning and impact of the medium in our daily lives.

*Read and carefully consider these perspectives. Each suggests a particular way of thinking about the impact of commercial television.*

| Perspective One | Perspective Two | Perspective Three |
| --- | --- | --- |
| Far from turning your brain to mush, commercial TV, watched judiciously, has much to offer modern society. TV provides a window on the world that is both instantaneous, vivid and informative. | Commercial television is responsible for the steep decline in high school test scores over the last two decades. TV disrupts narrative flow, shortens attention span and stunts intellectual development. | Commercial television is an evolving and diverse medium. Politics and news casts compete with reality shows and sit-coms. Equal parts entertainment and information, television seems to have something for everyone. |

> **Essay Task**
>
> Write a unified, coherent essay in which you evaluate multiple perspectives on the impact of commercial television. In your essay, be sure to:
>
> - analyze and evaluate the perspectives given
>
> - state and develop your own perspective on the issue
>
> - explain the relationship between your perspective and those given
>
> Your perspective may be in full agreement with any of the others, in partial agreement, or wholly different. Whatever the case, support your ideas with logical reasoning and detailed, persuasive examples.

## Isolate the Contrast

As usual, the prompt provides clear-cut pro and con positions on the topic, which you can cherry pick to get your essay started. Use a T-chart to state your positions and organize your sub-arguments. For example:

| **Pro** | **Con** |
| --- | --- |
| Modern TV is a positive influence because it provides a "window into society" as well as tools to educate. | TV distracts today's youth from critical analyses and fills their minds with pointless advertising. |
| **Sub-arguments** | |
| There are many educational shows that serve to inform the general public. For ex: Mickey Mouse Clubhouse. | Prevalence of "trash TV" can distort the viewpoint of teen-age youth. Reference Ebony magazine article. |
| TV shows like the Colbert Report provide cultural, political, and social commentary. | Teens are reading less classical literature because time spent in front of a TV screen is increasing. |
| | TV encourages rampant consumerism. |

Notice that some of the sub-arguments are drawn directly from the prompt, while others are the result of your imagination and analysis. Add concrete examples whenever possible to give yourself "talking points" as you develop your essay.

This T-chart acts as a roadmap to get you started down the road to a top-scoring essay. You'll flesh it out and embellish it as you go along.

**Perspectives**

Now address the main point of each of the perspectives provided below the prompt and attach concrete examples to support your positions. For example:

| Perspectives Chart |
|---|
| **Perspective 1**<br>Commercial television has much to offer modern society<br><br>CONCRETE EXAMPLES: Shows like "Mickey Mouse Clubhouse", the "View" and "Politically Incorrect" present a vivid and educational window on the world.<br><br>**Perspective 2**<br>Television disrupts attention spans and the emphasis on consumerism distracts teenagers from educational pursuits.<br><br>CONCRETE EXAMPLES: The "Real Housewives of Beverly Hills", Black Friday department store sales, decline in test scores.<br><br>**Perspective 3**<br>TV is increasing in its availability so it is still an evolving medium<br><br>CONCRETE EXAMPLES: The average teen spends about 30 hours a week in front of a screen. Additionally, more and more portable devices are being made on which TV shows can be broadcast. |

This chart is simply a means to organize the way you want to handle each of the given perspectives. Once you've mapped out your general arguments, feel free to enlarge upon your positions, add alternate explanations or introduce new concrete examples. The chart, like the T-chart, is a springboard to get you rolling on your essay.

## Sample Essay

*The Impact of Commercial Television*

Recently, the Kardashians made headlines when they renewed their hit TV show "Keeping Up with the Kardashians" for another three seasons at a whopping price of $40 million dollars. One has to look no further than the drunken family feuds and bad boy behavior that are displayed on the show to begin to wonder about where TV is headed. Critics from Ebony magazine, for example, lament that the rise of trash TV is here to stay, thus poisoning the youth of today with advertising and turning their focus away from classical literature. However, modern TV also provides an informative look at the cultural landscape of society. Although reality TV has yet to become a thing of the past, shows like Sesame Street and the Colbert Report, offer education in a form that is easy to digest. While it is crucial to acknowledge the downsides of modern television, for the most part what is presented on air gives us a glimpse of who we are today in addition to keeping people informed.

Television offers a plethora of shows that seek to educate children in an engaging way. As the child of a single mother, growing up I spent a lot of time watching children's shows such as Mickey Mouse Clubhouse and Reading Rainbow. These shows promoted literacy skills with segments that featured actors reading aloud books with voices that captivated. By making reading seem fun, TV shows can convince children from a young age to develop a lifelong love of reading. Later in life, television shows like "Politically Incorrect" or morning talk shows like "The View" can educate students on important political and cultural issues of the day. In this sense, TV can be an effective tool for educating viewers and impacting youth for the better. It provides a window on the world that is both instantaneous, vivid and informative.

On the other hand, much commercial television dwells on some of the most superficial and worst aspects of American culture. The yearly Black Friday sale that draws millions of Americans has led to the death of seven people and has injured more than 90. This rise of rampant consumerism is reflected and reinforced by shows like the "Real Housewives of Beverly Hills" where a group of women are shown in their lavish estates chock full of privileges that are only available to upper classes. This extreme form of consumerism and over consumption sends the wrong message to teenagers, distracting them from educational pursuits and dumbing down the culture. In fact, some critics claim that modern television is responsible for the steep decline in high school test scores over the last two decades. According to a study run by Dr. Barnett from the University of Montreal, teens spend an average of 30 hours a week sitting passively in front of a screen.

It seems clear that commercial television has something for everyone, both good and bad. On the one hand, today's TV can be viewed as an accurate source of information on cultural, political, and social issues. Furthermore, it can be used to encourage child development skills and important educational building blocks. However, when some forms of commercial TV are watched in excess, other sources of information, such as print literature, can lose value. With the increased availability of mobile viewing devices and the evolving nature of TV, only time will truly tell whether the positive benefits of modern television outweigh the negative impacts.

## Comments

Notice how Caiseen kicks off her essay with punch by citing a vivid, concrete example — the bad boy behavior of the Kardashians — in her intro. She follows that up with a critique from Ebony magazine that reinforces the idea of "trash TV". These introductory vignettes, or anecdotes, are important tools of a good writer.

Having set up one side of the contrast, Caiseen uses a transition word — however — to balance the narrative and broach an opposing viewpoint. Concrete examples of TV shows like Sesame Street and the Colbert Report lend substance to her argument.

Once the introductory contrasts are complete, Caiseen moves on to a sub-argument in her T-chart, using personal experience to demonstrate the educational value of such shows as Mickey Mouse Clubhouse. Implicit in this paragraph is the notion that TV has much to offer, which is the premise of Perspective Two. In fact, she concludes the paragraph by mentioning that TV "provides a window on the world", the same phrase used in the perspective, a neat trick to keep in mind while you're writing.

A concession paragraph follows that is devoted to the crass, commercial aspects of TV viewing. Advertisements for "Black Friday" sales and shows like "Real Housewives" are used as concrete examples of the extreme consumerism TV promotes. Finally, the steep decline in test scores, one of the main points in Perspective One, is reinforced.

Remember that it's essential to provide a concession paragraph of some sort on every ACT essay.

Finally, Caiseen folds a direct quote from Perspective Three into her conclusion, mentioning that commercial television has "something for everyone". She goes on to summarize her various arguments pro and con, ending with a reference to the evolving nature of the medium.

When developing your essay, a nice touch is to directly quote from one or more of the perspectives given. This lends credence to your arguments and demonstrates a logical progression.


## ACT Rubric in a Nutshell

You know the drill: to boil the ACT rubric down to its essentials, ask yourself the following questions:

* Does the essay express ideas and analysis relevant to the prompt?

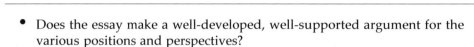

- Does the essay make a well-developed, well-supported argument for the various positions and perspectives?

- Is the essay organized in such a way as to lead the reader through the arguments in a logical and persuasive manner?

- Does the writer employ sentence variety, use transitions and supply sufficient detail to convey arguments with clarity and conviction?

By now you can answer these questions in your sleep. They should inform every ACT essay you write from now on.

# Different Sides of Multitasking

Nowadays individuals are bombarded with technology to the point that getting through the day means juggling multiple projects and media. Caie, a former student of mine who composed an essay on Intelligent Machines in Chapter 4, is back to lend her talents to another sample essay.

**Sample Prompt**

### Different Sides of Multitasking

A New York Times Magazine article asked in 2001: "Who can remember life before multitasking?" Indeed, the advent of faster technology means that most Americans today move from one project to another about every eleven minutes. Media multitasking — the simultaneous use of television, the Internet, video games, texts, and emails — has become prevalent in all aspects of American life, in many cases enhancing productivity and our ability to communicate. What, however, are the downsides to always focusing on multiple jobs at once? Do we lose our ability to concentrate when we are constantly bombarded with mixed media? Does this continuous shifting of our attention span make it difficult for us to set priorities and balance the demands of work, family and social life? Given the prevalence of multitasking in today's life, it is important to consider its true implications.

*Read and carefully consider these perspectives. Each suggests a particular way of thinking about multitasking.*

| Perspective One | Perspective Two | Perspective Three |
|---|---|---|
| Humans are meant to multitask. From an evolutionary perspective, behavioral flexibility is a natural consequence of larger, more complex brains. Multitasking allows us to maximize our own productivity as a species and accomplish more in a shorter amount of time. | When we try to focus on too many activities at once, we lose our ability to connect with those that actually matter most. The constant emphasis on our need to do multiple things at once only leads to lower productivity. Quality suffers when we try to accomplish too much. | The advent of technology challenges our perception of what it means to multitask. Does multitasking promote a mindset that encourages adaptability, accommodation, and compromise. Or does it produce information overload? |

| Essay Task |
|---|
| Write a unified, coherent essay in which you evaluate multiple perspectives on the different sides of multitasking. In your essay, be sure to:<br><br>• analyze and evaluate the perspectives given<br><br>• state and develop your own perspective on the issue<br><br>• explain the relationship between your perspective and those given<br><br>Your perspective may be in full agreement with any of the others, in partial agreement, or wholly different. Whatever the case, support your ideas with logical reasoning and detailed, persuasive examples. |

## Isolate the Contrasts

As usual, the prompt provides clear-cut pro and con positions on the topic, which you can cherry pick to get your essay started. Use a T-chart to state your positions and organize your sub-arguments. For example:

| Pro | Con |
|---|---|
| Multitasking is a way of life for many Americans today | Media overload is the potential downside of mixed media in modern life |

### Sub-arguments

| | |
|---|---|
| Increases productivity and enhances our ability to communicate | Decreases our attention span and creates imbalances in our daily lives |
| Diversity of media makes our life more interesting and less boring | Use Socrates example to show negative effects of information overload |

## Perspectives

Now address the main point of each of the perspectives provided and attach concrete examples to support your positions. For example:

≡

:

### Perspectives Chart

**Perspective 1**
Larger, more complex brains allow us to do multiple tasks at the same time

CONCRETE EXAMPLES:
Brain size matters. Monkeys vs Humans. Humans have a larger pre-frontal cortex. Cite MIT professor.

**Perspective 2**
When we try to focus on too many activities at once, we lose our ability to connect with those that actually matter most. Quality suffers.

CONCRETE EXAMPLES:
Michigan study. Texting and driving. Workplace anecdote.

**Perspective 3**
Technology promotes a multitasking mindset that encourages adaptability, accommodation, and compromise.

CONCRETE EXAMPLES:
Recap pros and cons in conclusion. Bring back Socrates. Can't have it all.

Again, once you've mapped out your general arguments, feel free to enlarge upon your positions, add alternate explanations or introduce new concrete examples. The chart is a springboard to get you rolling on your essay.

## Sample Essay

*Different Sides of Multitasking*

More than two thousand years ago, the Greek philosopher Socrates wrote that as the brain filled with noise – trivial information that did not matter in the larger picture – individuals lost their ability to focus on what was truly important. Socrates was speaking of the issues facing his time, including questions of democracy in Athens balanced by day-to-day worries about the state of his city. However, in today's context of constant communication with smartphones, computers, and social media, his ideas are even more relevant. On the one hand technology makes our lives more productive. On the other, as

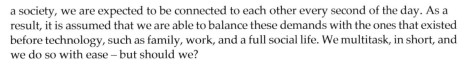

a society, we are expected to be connected to each other every second of the day. As a result, it is assumed that we are able to balance these demands with the ones that existed before technology, such as family, work, and a full social life. We multitask, in short, and we do so with ease – but should we?

From a psychological perspective, our constant focus on multitasking is beneficial, because it allows us to utilize a mental skill that sets us apart. The human brain is wired to help us switch and prioritize tasks. Monkeys, by contrast, have a much smaller brain size, and we can see our evolutionary advantage at work in our history. A large brain, in particular a large pre-frontal cortex, allows us to process large amounts of information quickly and efficiently.

On a more individual basis, if we were not able to focus on many things at once, we would not be able to balance differing schedules. Multitasking, in other words, encourages flexibility and accommodation. As MIT professor Daniel Weismann explains, "we can do more with our time through multitasking – we are not confined to a single duty but can switch and utilize all parts of our brain."

However, these advantages are too often viewed as positive factors, when in fact the opposite may be true. A study conducted at the University of Michigan looked at the relationship between texting and driving. When individuals attempted to switch between the two tasks, the experiment found that their reaction time was slower than when under the influence of alcohol or marijuana. Consider an anecdotal story about a worker constantly interrupted by phone calls, a vibrating phone, and changing demands from a boss. It's an experience not uncommon in today's workplace. Yet when we try to focus but are repeatedly stopped by other distractions, we find ourselves more frustrated and stressed but not more productive. In fact, the human brain cannot focus on two different activities simultaneously – we can only switch quickly from one task to another. But as we pile on the changes we need to make, we may force our brain to stretch in a way that results in exhaustion, rather than higher efficiency.

While it's true that multitasking promotes a mindset that encourages adaptability, accommodation, and compromise, we must not lose sight of its drawbacks. As Socrates warned all those years ago, when there is so much on our mind, we lose our ability to filter what is truly important. This understanding is perhaps most fundamental. While we like to think that we "can have it all," it may also be worth considering the implications of what that pursuit of continuous business actually means.

## Comments

Caie's intro, with great historical sweep, sets the stage for multitasking with an allusion to ancient Greece, where even great thinkers could lose their ability to focus. She then draws a parallel to today's world, parsing the prompt to show the pros and cons of technology and the way it affects and intrudes on our daily lives. She concludes with a rhetorical question that entreats us to consider the implications of multitasking. Excellent writing style and fine use of anecdote to set up context for the discussion.

Like Tina in a previous essay on photo-sharing, Caie uses a "psychological perspective" as both a transition from one paragraph to another and as an organizing construct for addressing Perspective 1. She uses brain size as an indicator of multitasking capabilities. She follows that up in the next paragraph by quoting an MIT professor to give objective support to her argument and cover one aspect on Perspective 3.

In her concession paragraph, Caie brings the discussion directly down to earth, citing a study that shows the negative relationship between texting and driving. Nice concrete example and good support for Perspective 2. She then doubles down on the drawbacks of multitasking using an anecdote of distractions in the workplace. Finally, she points out that multitasking may in fact result in reduced efficiency.

Having provided quotes, anecdotes, and citations to support her arguments, Caie is ready to conclude her essay by addressing the contrasts inherent in the prompt and the three perspectives. After taking words directly from Perspective 3 to summarize the positive aspects of multitasking, she returns to her intro to remind us of Socrates admonitions. A nice full-circle technique that leaves the final decision on the value of multitasking up the astute reader.

### ACT Rubric in a Nutshell

Here it is again for the last time, guys:

- Does the essay express ideas and analysis relevant to the prompt?
- Does the essay make a well-developed, well-supported argument for the various positions and perspectives?
- Is the essay organized in such a way as to lead the reader through the arguments in a logical and persuasive manner?
- Does the writer employ sentence variety, use transitions and supply sufficient detail to convey arguments with clarity and conviction?

Check, check, check and checkmate. Now go forth and write!

## What's Next

OK, by now you should understand the components that go into an outstanding essay and the questions that help you structure and compose it. In the final chapter, I'll provide you with several sample prompts that you can parse into T-charts in order to get busy producing your own *New ACT essays*.

# 7—Other Prompts

At some point, you may have wondered what the poem from T.S. Elliot in the Preface had to do with the rest of this book. Well, in this chapter we've come full circle, haven't we? We've explored the main themes of the new ACT: the prompt, the three perspectives, the sample essays. Now we arrive back where we started, at the prompt, and "know the place for the first time."

Having read through this book and seen the way it's done, you're ready now to do it on your own.

I'll supply four new prompts here as well as empty T-charts and Perspectives-charts so you can organize your thoughts "pro" and "con" in preparation for your essay. Time yourself and try to spend no more than 5 to10 minutes gathering your thoughts.

Then pick up your notebook (or use the lined paper at the end of this chapter) and start writing. Your goal is to include at least 450 words for a top-scoring essay. If you can't reach the 450 word limit the first time out, keep trying until you do. Remember, the essay is all about your ability to parse the prompt and evaluate the perspectives provided. Also remember to buttress your arguments with as many relevant details, details, details as possible in each body paragraph.

In your conclusion just wrap up and summarize everything you've written about. If possible, add a little contextual flourish at the end — a quote, an interesting observation, an anecdote or a personal reflection.

Once you've successfully covered the essay prompts in this chapter, search the net for other ACT prompts and keep working, keep practicing.

**Note:** Be sure to access the ACT website, where a second practice prompt was recently released entitled: "Public Health and Individual Freedom."

Here are the four new prompts provided in this chapter:

- Privacy vs Security
- Democratization of Information
- Value of Pets
- Football at a Crossroads

## ≡

# Privacy vs. Security

The first sample prompt and perspectives present issues surrounding surveillance devices.

## Sample Prompt

*Privacy vs. Security*

Many of the activities and obligations we fulfill daily are now monitored by automated cameras and other security devices. Governments around the world use mass surveillance technologies that have the capability of monitoring phone calls and broadband internet traffic. Many of the most popular sites we use everyday, despite their "privacy setting" option, contain within them sophisticated technologies that can track our most personal information. The growth of security and tracking technologies are generally seen as a sign of progress, but what is lost when we lose control of our own privacy on the Internet? Given the accelerating variety and prevalence of this type of surveillance, it is worth examining the implication and meaning of its presence in our lives.

*Read and carefully consider these perspectives. Each suggests a particular way of thinking about issues concerning privacy vs. security.*

| Perspective One | Perspective Two | Perspective Three |
|---|---|---|
| What we lose with the growth of tracking and surveillance technologies is some part of our own humanity. Even our mundane daily encounters may be monitored or used for other purposes, requiring from us no permission, consent, or basic courtesy. | Surveillance devices are good at promoting the security of our citizens. In fact, technology works better than humans at efficiently tracking dangerous activity and potential terrorism. This efficiency leads to a more prosperous and safe world for everyone. | Surveillance devices challenge our long-standing ideas about what safety and what personalized data-based information for all citizens can be. This is good because it pushes both humans and the devices we use toward new, unimagined possibilities. |

| Essay Task |
|---|
| Write a unified, coherent essay in which you evaluate multiple perspectives on the issues surrounding privacy vs. security. In your essay, be sure to:<br><br> • analyze and evaluate the perspectives given<br><br> • state and develop your own perspective on the issue<br><br> • explain the relationship between your perspective and those given<br><br>Your perspective may be in full agreement with any of the others, in partial agreement, or wholly different. Whatever the case, support your ideas with logical reasoning and detailed, persuasive examples. |

## Isolate the Contrast

OK, now it's your turn. Use the T-charts provided to parse the prompt, generate sub-arguments and analyze the perspectives to come up with a persuasive, well-written essay.

| Pro | Con |
|---|---|
| . | |

**Sub-arguments**

**Perspectives**

Now address the main point of each of the three perspectives provided and attach concrete examples to support your positions.

| Perspectives Chart |
|---|
| **Perspective 1**<br><br>CONCRETE EXAMPLES:<br><br>**Perspective 2**<br><br>CONCRETE EXAMPLES:<br><br>**Perspective 3**<br><br>CONCRETE EXAMPLES:<br><br> |

**Your Turn**

Take out a pad of lined paper (or use the blank pages provided at the end of this chapter) and compose a persuasive, well-argued essay. Remember, this chart is just a springboard to get you rolling on your essay. Feel free to adjust or add to your analysis during the actual writing.

# Democratization of Information

This sample prompt questions the advisability of unscreened information available to the public.

## Sample Prompt

### Democratization of Information

Consider for a moment how one receives information in the modern age — if a riot erupts in New York City, that news is immediately broadcasted over the Internet, where nothing is filtered. Some view this unscreened information as a step in the right direction — no information can be shielded from the public's eye, and so it is easier than ever to be well informed about what is truly occurring in the outside world. On the other hand, the uncensored nature of this constant flow can make it harder to decipher what is and is not important to see. If everything is publicized, what information is valuable? In addition, questions about journalistic integrity and privacy must be considered in this new information age. What facts belong in the public domain, and what should be considered private for security reasons? Because knowledge is easier than ever to garner, it is worthwhile to consider multiple sides of this argument.

*Read and carefully consider these perspectives. Each suggests a particular way of thinking about the uncensored flow of information.*

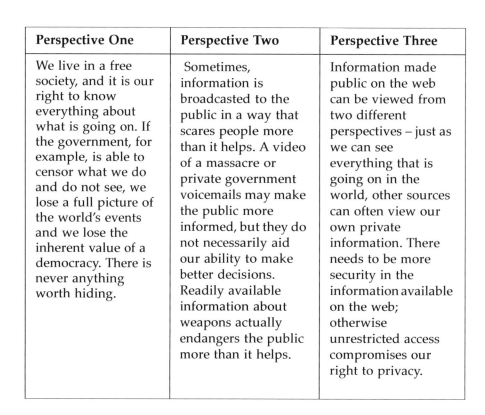

| Perspective One | Perspective Two | Perspective Three |
|---|---|---|
| We live in a free society, and it is our right to know everything about what is going on. If the government, for example, is able to censor what we do and do not see, we lose a full picture of the world's events and we lose the inherent value of a democracy. There is never anything worth hiding. | Sometimes, information is broadcasted to the public in a way that scares people more than it helps. A video of a massacre or private government voicemails may make the public more informed, but they do not necessarily aid our ability to make better decisions. Readily available information about weapons actually endangers the public more than it helps. | Information made public on the web can be viewed from two different perspectives – just as we can see everything that is going on in the world, other sources can often view our own private information. There needs to be more security in the information available on the web; otherwise unrestricted access compromises our right to privacy. |

| Essay Task |
|---|
| Write a unified, coherent essay in which you evaluate multiple perspectives on the increasing presence of intelligent machines. In your essay, be sure to: |

| Essay Task |
| --- |
| Write a unified, coherent essay in which you evaluate multiple perspectives on the issues surrounding privacy vs. security. In your essay, be sure to:<br><br>• analyze and evaluate the perspectives given<br><br>• state and develop your own perspective on the issue<br><br>• explain the relationship between your perspective and those given<br><br>Your perspective may be in full agreement with any of the others, in partial agreement, or wholly different. Whatever the case, support your ideas with logical reasoning and detailed, persuasive examples. |

**Isolate the Contrast**

OK, now it's your turn. Use the T-charts provided to parse the prompt, generate sub-arguments and analyze the perspectives to come up with a persuasive, well-written essay.

| Pro | Con |
| --- | --- |
| . | |

**Sub-arguments**

**Perspectives**

Now address the main point of each of the three perspectives provided and attach concrete examples to support your positions.

| Perspectives Chart |
|---|
| **Perspective 1** |
| CONCRETE EXAMPLES: |
| **Perspective 2** |
| CONCRETE EXAMPLES: |
| **Perspective 3** |
| CONCRETE EXAMPLES: |

**Your Turn**

Take out a pad of lined paper (or use the blank pages provided at the end of this chapter) and compose a persuasive, well-argued essay. You know the drill.

# Value of Pets

This sample prompt questions the role pets play in social interaction.

## Sample Prompt

*Value of Pets*

The idea that a dog is a "man's best friend" is an old and familiar adage. Yet the saying is backed up by truth - substantial research suggests that pets have therapeutic benefits that cannot be understated. They promote social interaction, reduce stress, encourage exercise, and most importantly for many, provide unconditional love and affection. Moreover, pets teach responsibility, because they require work and attention just like all members of a family. However, there is some evidence that pets can also come to replace human connection – that people turn to their animals as sources of loyalty and inadvertently replace their real-life social interaction with a reliance on an animal. In addition, pets for a compromised owner, perhaps one facing serious life issues or aging, can come to represent real sources of stress. In light of these considerations, it is important to evaluate the popular narrative of the value of a pet, in order to reach a fuller conclusion about their impact on our lives.

*Read and carefully consider these perspectives. Each suggests a particular way of thinking about the value of pets.*

| Perspective One | Perspective Two | Perspective Three |
|---|---|---|
| After a long day of work or a tough situation in one's personal life, there is an immeasurable value in having a pet on which one can rely. Because many pets require care, they encourage a more active and routine lifestyle for their owners. Their consistent needs can in turn provide a stability that is often difficult to find. | Pets cost money, and because the evidence for their value is often anecdotal rather than statistical, they only add a financial burden to their owner. With a full schedule, an animal that requires attention, maintenance, and money is not always a positive option. | Pets can sometimes come to replace real human relationships. Because they are capable of providing unconditional love, some research suggests that pet owners expect these qualities to be true in the rest of their lives. |

---

| Essay Task |
| --- |
| Write a unified, coherent essay in which you evaluate multiple perspectives on the value of pets. In your essay, be sure to:<br><br>• analyze and evaluate the perspectives given<br><br>• state and develop your own perspective on the issue<br><br>• explain the relationship between your perspective and those given<br><br>Your perspective may be in full agreement with any of the others, in partial agreement, or wholly different. Whatever the case, support your ideas with logical reasoning and detailed, persuasive examples. |

### Isolate the Contrast

OK, now it's your turn. Use the T-charts provided to parse the prompt, generate sub-arguments and analyze the perspectives to come up with a persuasive, well-written essay.

| Pro | Con |
| --- | --- |
| | |

**Sub-arguments**

### Perspectives

Now address the main point of each of the three perspectives provided and attach concrete examples to support your positions.

| Perspectives Chart |
| --- |
| **Perspective 1**<br><br>CONCRETE EXAMPLES:<br><br>**Perspective 2**<br><br>CONCRETE EXAMPLES:<br><br>**Perspective 3**<br><br>CONCRETE EXAMPLES: |

### Your Turn

As usual, take out a pad of lined paper (or use the blank pages provided at the end of this chapter) and compose a persuasive, well-argued essay. You should be getting better at this by now!

# Football at a Crossroads

This sample prompt considers the health issues associated with football.

## Sample Prompt

*Football at a Crossroad*

The cover of a recent TIME magazine feature reads: "He died playing this game. Is football worth it?" There is no question that football, a longtime all-American obsession, is a dangerous game, but recently, growing numbers of traumatic brain injuries have brought into light the life-threatening nature of the sport. Researchers at the Colorado School of Public Health found that football had the highest incidence of brain-rattling impacts. Yet the sport is also one rooted in our culture – the NFL annually garners revenue that tops all U.S. professional sports leagues. Is there a way to combat the danger while keeping the pastime alive? Is football just too harmful? Given the prevalence of football in so many Americans' lives, it is important to consider the concerns of safety while acknowledging the value of the game.

| Perspective One | Perspective Two | Perspective Three |
|---|---|---|
| There is a way to balance concerns about safety without losing the integrity of the game. The reality is that it's impossible to play football without getting hit. Consequently, Physical contact is an essential part of the sport. | For too long the danger of the football has been underestimated. Athletes who suffer concussions are on the rise. Injuries may be incapacitated for life. Others may experience debilitating injuries that detract from the quality of life. | American football is a national and historic pastime. Some balance must be struck to minimize physical injuries endured by players while maintaining the individual and social benefits of the sport. |

| Essay Task |
|---|
| Write a unified, coherent essay in which you evaluate multiple perspectives on the value of pets. In your essay, be sure to: <br><br> • analyze and evaluate the perspectives given <br><br> • state and develop your own perspective on the issue <br><br> • explain the relationship between your perspective and those given <br><br> Your perspective may be in full agreement with any of the others, in partial agreement, or wholly different. Whatever the case, support your ideas with logical reasoning and detailed, persuasive examples. |

## Isolate the Contrast

OK, now it's your turn. Use the T-charts provided to parse the prompt, generate sub-arguments and analyze the perspectives to come up with a persuasive, well-written essay.

| Pro | Con |
|---|---|
| | |

**Sub-arguments**

## Perspectives

Now address the main point of each of the three perspectives provided and attach concrete examples to support your positions.

| Perspectives Chart |
| --- |
| **Perspective 1** |
| CONCRETE EXAMPLES: |
| **Perspective 2** |
| CONCRETE EXAMPLES: |
| **Perspective 3** |
| CONCRETE EXAMPLES: |

### Your Turn

As usual, take out a pad of lined paper (or use the blank pages provided at the end of this chapter) and compose a persuasive, well-argued essay. At this point, piece of cake, right!

## Parting Thoughts

Just so you know, further help is on the way. In September of this year (2015), I'll distribute a short but comprehensive Youtube workshop covering the essentials of ACT essay writing. The workshop comprises the following three segments:

- The Prompt
- Three Perspectives
- Sample Essay

You can access the video at: www.youtube.com/tctutoring

Visit my website for more info: www.tctutoring.net

Good luck with your essay, with college, with life!

98